The 10% Entrepreneur

'For four years, while working a full time job, I was also a 10% Entrepreneur. I didn't know the phrase then, I just knew I had more money, more fun and more opportunities than I'd ever had in my life. If any of those sound like things you want more of, read this book' Jon Acuff, author of *Do Over*

'Entrepreneurship is not one size fits all. It can take many shapes and forms. There's immense value to testing ideas or weaving entrepreneurial qualities into your life before taking the plunge. *The 10% Entrepreneur* will tell you how' Christine Tsai, founding partner of 500 Startups

'We think of entrepreneurship as a big, scary thing, involving blind leaps of faith and sweeping acts of disruption, not for the faint of heart. Yet in today's ever-changing world, everyone needs to act more like an entrepreneur and take risks – or risk being left behind. In his debut book, McGinnis delivers a winning game-plan for assuming 10 per cent more risk, more creativity and more (ad)venture in your everyday life for 100 per cent more satisfaction. Entrepreneurship is a smart choice for everyone – and so is reading this book' Linda Rottenberg, co-founder and CEO of Endeavor and author of *Crazy is a Compliment*

'In a shifting corporate landscape, entrepreneurship no longer has to mean all-or-nothing endeavours. Patrick McGinnis uses his own expertise as a "part-time entrepreneur" to illustrate a proven solution for you to become one, too' Keith Ferrazzi, author of *Who's Got Your Back* and *Never Eat Alone*

ABOUT THE AUTHOR

Patrick J. McGinnis is a venture capitalist and private equity investor who founded Dirigo Advisors, after a decade on Wall Street, to provide strategic advice to investors, entrepreneurs and fast-growing businesses. He is also a 10% entrepreneur, investing in, advising and launching a diverse portfolio of companies and investments in the United States, Latin America and Asia. A graduate of Harvard Business School, he writes for *Business Insider*, the *Huffington Post*, *Boston Magazine* and *Forbes*. He lives in New York City.

The 10% Entrepreneur

Live Your Startup Dream
Without Quitting Your Day Job

Patrick J. McGinnis

PORTFOLIO
PENGUIN

PORTFOLIO PENGUIN

UK | USA | Canada | Ireland | Australia
India | New Zealand | South Africa

Portfolio Penguin is part of the Penguin Random House group of companies
whose addresses can be found at global.penguinrandomhouse.com

First published in the United States of America by Portfolio/Penguin,
a member of Penguin Group (USA) Inc. 2016
First published in Great Britain by Portfolio Penguin 2016

001

Printed in Great Britain by Clays Ltd, St Ives plc

A CIP catalogue record for this book is available from the British Library

ISBN: 978–0–241–19878–0

www.greenpenguin.co.uk

Penguin Random House is committed to a
sustainable future for our business, our readers
and our planet. This book is made from Forest
Stewardship Council® certified paper.

To all my teachers — especially my parents

Contents

Introduction   1

Part 1. Why Should You Be a 10% Entrepreneur?

Chapter 1. One Job Is Not Enough   11

Chapter 2. All the Benefits Without the Pitfalls   27

Chapter 3. The Five Types of 10% Entrepreneurs   41

Part 2. Building Your 10%

Chapter 4. What Kind of 10% Entrepreneur Are You?   63

Chapter 5. Making the Most of Time and Money   77

Chapter 6. Playing to Your Strengths   93

Chapter 7. Finding, Analyzing, and Committing to Ventures   115

Chapter 8. Building Your Team   147

Contents

Chapter 9. Overcoming Obstacles 173

Chapter 10. Winning the Long Game 185

Acknowledgments 203

Glossary 207

Appendix 209

Notes 215

Index 219

Introduction

Are you ready to become a 10% Entrepreneur?

If you've been following the rapid changes in technology, opportunity, and mind-set that are reshaping the global economy, then you've probably noticed that a movement is taking form. Everywhere you look, people are embracing entrepreneurship, flexibility, and autonomy as never before, even while holding down full-time corporate jobs. A recent college graduate is starting his own lobster-roll empire, a designer is running a thriving children's clothing company, and a group of friends from Bible study are building a craft beer company, all on a part-time basis. For them, entrepreneurship is a choice that is additive, rather than absolute, and it offers upside opportunity and downside protection, all while making their lives richer and more interesting. Why shouldn't the same apply to you?

What does it mean to be a 10% Entrepreneur? You will invest at least 10% of your time and, if possible, 10% of your capital into new investments and opportunities. By leveraging your base of experience and your network, you will choose opportunities that play to your strengths and that are complementary to your career and your interests. Most important, you will be the owner of everything you create. You may change your career at multiple points in a lifetime, changing functions, changing roles, and changing companies, but you'll always be creating value for the most important employer of all: you.

Let me make something very clear from the outset. This book is not anticorporate or antijob. In fact, it's quite the opposite. Over the course of the next ten chapters, you will learn how you can remain completely committed to your job while acquiring new skills that will make you even more effective at the office. After all, there are lots of reasons to appreciate your day job. It provides a place for you to learn, network, take risks, and contribute to a team. You enjoy opportunities for advancement, education, and social interaction. All those things are invaluable, without mentioning the blindingly obvious reason to appreciate your job: it pays you a steady salary plus benefits. None of those considerations should be taken for granted, but as I learned the hard way, you also need to look for more.

My journey toward becoming a 10% Entrepreneur began when I was a vice president at an emerging-markets investment fund. I invested in venture capital and private equity deals all over the world, which meant that I was constantly zigzagging around the globe and working with companies in places like Pakistan, Colombia, the United Arab Emirates, Poland, Turkey, China, and the Philippines. Other than the fact that I lived in a state of permanent jet lag, I loved my job. It was the perfect combination of travel, intellectual stimulation, and financial rewards. It was also the kind of life that allowed for more than a few James Bond moments. Maybe I took the subway to work in New York, but in Istanbul or Karachi or Bogotá, I mixed with serious power players who sailed their yachts to dinner or circulated with armed guards in bulletproof SUVs.

Perhaps it was all that jet lag, but the onset of the global financial meltdown in the autumn of 2008 caught me completely off guard. Even as I sat in my office on Park Avenue watching the crisis unfold on CNBC, I didn't quite get how all those changes might affect me. Until they did. Unfortunately, my investment fund just happened to sit within a division of AIG. Yes, that AIG, the one that in the wake of the financial crisis made a reliable target for late-night comedians, picketing protesters, and just about everyone else. It was the company about which Congressman Paul Hodes of New Hampshire declared, "I think AIG now stands for arrogance, incompetence and greed."[1] Ouch, that one still stings a little.

Even though the writing was on the wall, I couldn't process what was happening. It didn't make sense. AIG wasn't some bold, sexy hedge fund. It was a boring insurance company with a trillion-dollar balance sheet. A trillion dollars! What could go wrong?

It turns out, a lot. Even a trillion dollars couldn't save AIG once there was blood in the water. It didn't matter that my division of the company had nothing to do with the risky investments that took the business down. In the space of days, the U.S. government announced a plan to effectively nationalize the company. In an instant, everything changed. Rather than working for a trillion-dollar business, I was now essentially a ward of the state. Upon hearing the news, I fired up my laptop and updated my

Facebook status: "Patrick McGinnis is proud to be working for you—the American taxpayer."

That's when things got interesting. When I woke up the next day, something occurred to me. Although my firm would probably never be the same, and my future there was unclear, I was still alive and kicking. In fact, I felt strangely liberated. So much so that I resolved to question everything I thought I knew about building a career. I spent the next few months trying to make sense of it all, but I kept coming back to the same question: Where had I gone wrong? Over time, I realized that the answer was staring me in the face: I had naively expected the safety and security of one company to provide everything I needed. Unfortunately for me, that stability was an illusion.

I consider myself lucky. Absent the financial crisis, I would have plugged along, head down, eyes forward, on the same set path. I thought my career was bulletproof since I had done everything by the book and had an MBA from Harvard. I was mistaken. Instead I was now the guy who'd built his entire career with the express purpose of avoiding failure but, in fact, had just failed rather spectacularly. It took AIG's stock crashing, both literally and figuratively, to shake me from my complacency.

There was still one big problem. I was completely at a loss regarding my next move. Having advanced through the first decade of my career in a series of step functions, I had never bothered to formulate a Plan B. But there was some good news, too. I was now free to find a different and far more interesting path. All I knew for certain was that I would never again bet the entirety of my career on the fate of one company. Apart from that, the horizon was wide open and I had very little to lose. I'd played it safe in the past and look how that turned out, so maybe it was time to embrace a little risk and even consider entrepreneurship.

Yet after some soul-searching, I concluded that I couldn't really see myself becoming a full-fledged entrepreneur, at least not in the foreseeable future. I didn't have any great ideas and I didn't want to give up the stability of having a day job. I also didn't really *feel* like an entrepreneur.

For the first decade of my career I viewed entrepreneurship as something for other people, but not for me. I was someone who exclusively sought the well-traveled path, worked for large corporations, and saw myself solidly fitting the mold of a "company man." That was enough. I expended too much energy working at one firm to consider adding to my workload. When I talked to friends who were taking part in new ventures outside of work, I smiled, thinking, "Why on earth would you want to spend your free time working?"

Then there was the question of risk. Entrepreneurship was a viable option for some people, but I grew up in small-town America and was terrified of failure. If I struck out on Wall Street, there was no inheritance waiting for me to fall back on, only a life lived in my parents' basement. So what if it was a finished basement with a half bath and cable television? I didn't want to give up the prestige, and most important the paycheck, of a stable job for something that wasn't a sure bet. I was very happy being a 0% Entrepreneur and I wanted to work for the biggest and safest company out there.

The financial crisis changed everything. As I struggled to plot my next steps, I decided that I needed to create a new type of career that would be achievable as well as sustainable. What would be the point of making changes that would be too difficult or too radical to actually put into practice? If I was going to go back to the drawing board, I needed to be realistic. Rather than becoming an entrepreneur, perhaps I could find a way to work entrepreneurship into my career without abandoning the concept of a day job. Maybe I'd had it backward all along. Instead of thinking of entrepreneurship as something that was inherently risky, it could actually be my insurance policy.

In the very early days, when I was first starting to think about this incremental, more pragmatic approach to entrepreneurship, I talked to friends and even acquaintances about my idea. Pretty soon, I sat next to a guy on a plane who had invested some cash in a toy company. Then I heard that a friend was spending weekends working on a new fashion brand both as an investor and in exchange for free stock. I also learned that a former colleague was leveraging her credibility in the tech scene to advise startups all over the world. These were some of the first 10% Entrepreneurs I met, and although I didn't quite know how to describe what they were doing, one thing was clear: all of these people were onto something.

As I grew convinced that I wanted to somehow become a 10% Entrepreneur, I was also consumed with doubt. I found myself grappling with a growing list of questions. How should I begin? How would I know what to do? Did I have sufficient time and money to dedicate to making it happen? How risky was it going to be? Did I have the judgment and the experience to make good decisions?

Now, five years later, having answered these questions for myself, I firmly believe that 10% Entrepreneurs are not born, they're made, and you can learn, just as I did. Like all the people you will meet in this book, I have built a portfolio of professional activities that reflects my skills, interests, and relationships. All told, I have invested a combination of time and money in twelve entrepreneurial ventures. In seven of these instances, my ownership stake is either partly or entirely the result of an investment of time, which is commonly known as sweat equity, rather than money.

By relying on a clear methodology to select investments and build my portfolio, I've made real money while creating significant upside for the future. To date, I've realized nearly two times my investment in cash, and the market value of my remaining holdings exceeds ten times my initial investment. I also participated in three real estate projects that provide long-term upside as well as current income in the form of cash dividends. In addition to making profitable investments, I've had a lot of fun and I've worked with some fantastic people, some of whom you'll meet later on. It's been a tremendous experience that fundamentally changed the way I think about my career. In fact, I have just one regret: Why didn't I start before? If I'd woken up the day after the implosion of AIG with a portfolio of investments to provide me with safe passage until my life and my career stabilized, the entire experience would have been far less fraught and painful. Rather than mourning what I lost, I would have been able to direct my energies into something positive—my 10%.

The good news is that there's no time like the present. This book will give you the tools and the game plan to integrate entrepreneurship into your career. It also contains the very kind of advice that I wish someone had imparted to me years ago. The first section, "Why Should You Be a 10% Entrepreneur?," sets the context for the 10% movement and explains the compelling reasons why so many people are integrating entrepreneurship into their careers. It will also introduce the five types of 10% Entrepreneurs. The second section, "Building Your 10%," will provide you with a step-by-step guide to formulating a strategy that will launch you into the next phase of your career.

Throughout this book you will meet real-life 10% Entrepreneurs who come from all over the world, operate in a range of industries, and bring different core skills to the table. They include a designer, a software engineer, a literary agent, a car salesman, an infomercial producer, a doctor, a stay-at-home parent, some students, and a few lawyers, as well as people working in finance, consulting, tech, and a variety of corporate roles. Despite their differences, these individuals have all employed similar approaches to launch and manage their 10%, and their strategies are entirely replicable—you can study them and then apply them yourself.

Pursuing entrepreneurship on the side is a choice that is pragmatic rather than theoretical, so it's not just a cool idea that you'll never actually pull off in real life. You don't need an MBA, a law degree, or any other specialized degree to understand and implement the game plan in this book. You also don't need twenty years of experience, millions in the bank, or to be living in New York City or San Francisco or London. You just need confidence in your own abilities, a willingness to look for help when necessary, and the tools to get started.

Part 1

Why Should You Be a 10% Entrepreneur?

Chapter 1

One Job Is Not Enough

Complacency isn't something that happens overnight. No one gets out of bed in the morning, looks in the mirror and thinks, "I guess I'll be complacent," then shrugs and heads back to bed. Instead, it creeps up on you. Early in my career, I accepted a job that I knew was not going to be a good fit. When I signed the offer letter, the knot in my stomach confirmed my doubts, but I had no other options and I needed to deal with a mountain of student debt. By my third month on the job, when I took a 45-minute nap under my desk in the middle of the afternoon, I realized I'd grown dangerously complacent. The next day, I started a job search and soon made the fateful move to AIG.

Later, in the aftermath of the global financial crisis, I found that it wasn't so easy to move on to another job. In the post-apocalyptic economy, I was basically trapped at AIG. Rather than doing something productive or just taking a siesta, this time I opted for petulance. I removed all signs of life from my office, taking books, notebooks, even pictures off the surface of the desk and putting them into cabinets and drawers until the glassed-in room looked completely empty from the hall. In essence, I erased myself from the workplace in a symbolic gesture that I sarcastically referred to as the "clean sweep."

At this very moment, complacency is pervasive in the American workplace. Even if you're not snoring under your desk or taking the passive-aggressive route like I did, you may very well be checked out. A 2015 Gallup study of the state of the American workplace found that nearly 70 percent of people are either "not engaged" or are "actively disengaged." By my count, that means that tens of millions of workers might as well be doing the "clean sweep," because their heads are not in the game.

When Sure Bets Are No Longer Sure

It's not surprising that so many people are sleepwalking their way through their professional lives. Climbing the corporate ladder is not the barometer of career achievement that it once was. Instead, it's yesterday's dream. At a time when the global economy oscillates from one economic crisis to another with disturbing regularity, few people expect to stick around a company long enough to collect a gold watch upon retirement. Economic cycles aside, it's nearly impossible to plan for the future thanks to the merging, offshoring, outsourcing, and downsizing that continually reshape the contours of the modern workplace.

The U.S. Bureau of Labor Statistics reports that the average member of the baby-boomer generation changed jobs every 3.5

years between the ages of twenty-two and forty-four.[1] This trend looks set to accelerate: 91 percent of millennials expect to stay no more than three years in a particular job. At that pace, a typical worker will bounce around twenty or so times in the course of a career.[2] Put simply, the old meritocratic mind-set through which many of us were taught to view our careers—"work hard, keep your head down, and move ahead"—no longer applies in a world where looking to grab on to the next rung of the ladder is not a viable strategy.

Even the traditional paradigms of prestige, paths like finance, law, and medicine, are no longer guaranteed to lead to financial success. There are no sure things, and it's not just because of the damage caused by the 2008 global financial crisis. In the last five years, the number of "front office" employees at Wall Street firms, people like investment bankers and traders, fell by 20 percent globally, while changes in pay structures and a heavy increase in regulation greatly affected compensation.[3] Things are no better in the legal and medical professions. Only 40 percent of 2010 law school graduates work in law firms and approximately 20 percent work in jobs that do not require a law license.[4] Perhaps that's why a recent survey found that roughly 60 percent of practicing lawyers would not advise young people to enter the industry.[5] Similarly, only 54 percent of doctors said they would choose medicine again if they started over.[6]

If you can't make it in the industries that were supposed to be no-brainers for success, then what does that say about the rest of the job market? The fact that there are no sure bets is not lost on the next wave of would-be professionals. Why go to school for years and rack up vast sums of student loans when the payout is no longer certain? It's a lousy deal and the best and brightest know it. As a result, they want more than your average sit-in-a-cubicle, work-your-way-up-for-twenty-years type of office job. For them, the answer is entrepreneurship.

Visit a college campus today and you will run across many more aspiring Mark Zuckerbergs than aspiring investment bankers, even though bankers were traditionally said to be the "Masters of the Universe." It's not just that Zuckerberg can wear jeans and a hoodie to work and is way richer, although that doesn't hurt. Entrepreneurial companies provide the kind of setting in which people who are just a few years out of school can build careers that combine autonomy and financial upside, all within a corporate culture that appeals to their values. They can also acquire the tools to someday launch an entrepreneurial venture of their own, if they so choose. Who can blame them for being attracted to this new paradigm? As technology disrupts and transforms even the most established industries seemingly overnight, thinking like an entrepreneur is now essential.

Entrepreneurship, Inc.

Unfortunately, thinking like an entrepreneur has little to do with the Hollywood version of entrepreneurship that has captured the public's imagination. Just as the 1980s had Gordon Gecko, *Wall Street*, and "Greed is good," we now have *The Social Network* and HBO's *Silicon Valley*. In that sense, entrepreneurs, like yuppies or hipsters before them, have become a type. With the passing of each year, they somehow manage to generate newfound levels of hype. Flip through a magazine focused on entrepreneurship or read a few startup blogs and you'll discover that nearly everyone is portrayed as independent, brilliant, edgy, and so innovative that they are beyond reproach. The message is unambiguous: entrepreneurs are the new pioneers, a fearless army of visionary warriors who will make untold sums of money. They will own the future.

What you are witnessing is something I like to call "Entrepreneurship, Inc." Thanks to a combination of creativity and chutzpah, the people responsible for Entrepreneurship, Inc., have done a remarkable job of productizing and branding a human endeavor that has far more to do with hard work than with glamour. As a result, society has embraced a distorted and romanticized notion of what it means to build a business from the ground up. The entrepreneurship-industrial complex knows that showing the real nature of starting a company is lousy product positioning, and telling people to work harder isn't alluring. The truth is that entrepreneurship is an all-consuming career choice, and unless you are a masochist, there is nothing particularly romantic about failing over and over again until you find the right formula.

It doesn't help that companies themselves muddy the water through their origin stories. It seems like every new venture was dreamed up in a garage, a dorm room, or while contemplating the sunset from a beach in Thailand. Telling those origin stories is far more inspiring than admitting that you came up with your startup idea while sitting in a poorly lit cubicle somewhere in Ohio.[7] Take the legend behind Apple. The California garage where Steve Wozniak and Steve Jobs started Apple is now a pilgrimage site. Aspiring founders and Apple fanboys take selfies out front. That makes Apple the world's most successful product of the classic Silicon Valley garage story. Except it isn't. In 2014,

Wozniak admitted that the whole garage story was a "bit of a myth," since the "actual work was being done . . . at my cubicle at Hewlett-Packard."[8]

The vast majority of founders are more obsessed with results than with feeding the entrepreneurship frenzy—and with good reason. If you are an entrepreneur and you believe your own hype, your investors should show you the door before you lose all their money. It's dangerous to take your eye off the ball and waste valuable time and energy reveling in your awesomeness. You may look the part and talk the talk, but results are what drive the value of any company when all is said and done. Looking the part without doing the work is a surefire way to end up being a first class "wantrepreneur."

That's what's so unfortunate about the glorification of entrepreneurship. Glossing over the substance to focus on flash leaves one critical factor out of the conversation: full-time entrepreneurship is not for everyone. There is no shame in deciding that you don't want to be an entrepreneur today—or ever! In fact, choosing a more structured path may be one of the best and most important decisions you ever make. Jumping from a stable career into something that is risky and in which you are unsure of yourself shouldn't be done recklessly. You need to go in with your eyes open.

Five Reasons Not to Be a Full-time Entrepreneur

My brother, Mike, is a jazz musician in New York City. Over the years, he has invested countless hours developing his skills and his reputation in the music scene. In the process, he's lugged his saxophone all over New York and all over the world, gradually moving up in his industry and making a name for himself. If you ask him why he chose to be a musician, his answer is simple: music chose him. That was the only thing he ever wanted to do, and he made the necessary sacrifices to pursue his passion, especially in the early days of his career when he could barely pay the bills. With success, he's found that he can live a much better life than he might have imagined a decade back. Perhaps he'll even strike it rich someday. Still, if he were looking for fame and money, he would have chosen a different path. He once told me that he sees being an artist today as akin to being a person of the cloth. You're doing it for passion, not for money, and in that sense, you've already struck it rich.

I see entrepreneurship in much the way that my brother sees a career in music. You don't become an entrepreneur because you want to be rich or famous. You become an entrepreneur because it chooses you. No matter when you make the decision, you know in your gut that you just have to go for it. Perhaps you're the person who has been launching businesses since you set up your first lemonade stand at the age of five. Maybe you knew from the outset that you were never going to work for anyone else. Or you didn't expect to be an entrepreneur, but you reached a stage in life where you wanted to live differently than you had in the past. Regardless of how you get there, when you choose entrepreneurship, you accept that the success and the money are terrific if they come, but they cannot be the only drivers of your decision.

Despite all the hype from Entrepreneurship, Inc., it is too hard a road to travel if you do so for the wrong reasons, or without thinking long and hard about what lies ahead. If you're considering that road, you should first think through these five perfectly rational reasons not to be a 100% Entrepreneur.

1. The Lifestyle Is Lousy

In September 2014, an entrepreneur named Ali Mese published a post on Medium titled "How quitting my corporate job for my startup dream f*cked my life up." Mese, a former Bain & Company consultant, chronicled the unexpected personal, familial, and social stresses that resulted from his decision to leave the safe and prestigious world of management consulting to start his own company. Having been caught off guard himself, Mese wanted to make sure that all the bored consultants, understimulated corporate types, and frustrated bankers who dreamed about startups from their cubicles also saw the other, darker side of Entrepreneurship, Inc., so he laid it bare. Clearly, the risks and trade-offs of pursuing entrepreneurship are on a lot of people's minds—his blog went viral, racking up millions of views.

The time and focus required to launch and lead a company takes a toll on you and everyone in your life. You have to rethink your financial goals, your lifestyle, and your definition of success, all while being plagued with self-doubt. It's generally believed that divorce rates among startup founders are the highest of any occupation, as a result of the long hours and stress.

Even if your company thrives, your lifestyle may not be luxurious. If you leave your corporate law job to open a bakery and finally make a business out of your grandmother's famous cookie recipe, you may find yourself working far more hours for a fraction of the pay. Sure, you have "freedom," but you also have long hours, demanding clients, and the stress of making ends meet on less money, at least at the outset. Lives, like careers, are rarely in balance, and you may find that your "dream job" has even less equilibrium than your previous job. After all the hard work and sacrifice, how terrible would it feel if you opened your bakery only to discover that you should have stayed at the law firm? It took you going all in to realize that while you enjoyed baking a few batches of cookies for your friends, you hate doing it twelve hours a day.

2. You Can Ruin Your Finances

A recent study of more than ten thousand founders revealed that 73 percent of respondents pay themselves less than $50,000 a year in cash compensation.[9] Those figures are surprisingly low when you consider how much responsibility they carry on their shoulders. They recruit teams, craft and execute growth strategies, and try to raise millions of dollars of venture capital from deep pocketed investors who expect the founders to make them richer. All those pressures and obligations for less than $50,000 a year sounds like a raw deal, right?

It may sound like a raw deal, but that is generally *the* deal. Investors expect startup founders to put all their eggs in one basket and make money as the value of their shares in a company increase. Now consider that the typical venture capital–backed business takes between five and seven years to go from raising its first round of capital to producing returns for its shareholders, including the founders.[10] Even Facebook, one of the undisputed tech heavyweights of the last decade, took more than seven years to reach its IPO.[11] So even if your company is wildly successful, you're going to have to wait to see the payoff.

Jonathan Olsen, an entrepreneur who's both founded and invested in early-stage ventures, puts it best: "If you want to be an entrepreneur, you have to give up things, starting with your flat-screen TV." Beyond the TV, you may no longer be in a position to help out your parents with unexpected costs and you won't be writing eye-popping checks to your alma mater. If you've gotten used to being the one who takes care of those around you, having to count every penny is not an insignificant change. Everyone likes to tell stories about the founder who ran down his savings and lived off multiple credit cards before finally making it big. No one talks about the founder who couldn't repay those bills.

3. You're Abandoning Status and Affirmation

Your job denotes your place in society and a prestigious career brings respect and affirmation from your colleagues, your family, and your friends. If everyone knows you as that guy who makes a lot of money in finance or that woman who is next up to make partner, then you might have grown accustomed to being seen in a certain light. Changes in your career affect the way you are perceived by your peers, society, and even yourself. Endangering this affirmation can mess with your head.

If you've worked for an established company, you are used to the security and structure that are woven into the DNA of those types of organizations. Pursuing new opportunities means breaking routines and leaving behind old comforts. Once the thrill of liberation wanes, abandoning well-appointed corporate offices for startup digs means that you will have to get used to doing all kinds of grunt work. Say good-bye to nice hotels and expense account dinners. You'll also trade in your business cards for new ones, leaving behind a well-known corporate logo in exchange for a card that elicits looks of confusion. Finally, you'll have to learn to swallow your pride. At some point, you're going to be pitching your business to people who sit in the very comfortable corporate offices that you left behind. Some of them, maybe most of them, are going to say, "No, thank you."

Even if you see yourself as someone who is independent, who doesn't look for approval from others, and who knows what you want, the transition can be trying. Most of your old friends and colleagues will have no idea what you're doing for a living, so explaining yourself to people will not be as easy as it once was. When you do, some people will look at you skeptically while others will struggle to keep their eyes from glazing over. These people may include members of your family.

4. You Don't Have the Right Idea (Yet)

I was standing in the corner at a tech networking event when an excited young man stormed up to me. He had just come from a hackathon, a business plan competition in which teams of aspiring entrepreneurs work around the clock to develop an idea that could actually become a business. Tired but triumphant, he wanted to tell me about the mobile app he'd hatched with his team. Specifically, he wanted to know if he should drop out of college and throw all his energy into something he'd only just dreamed up. He caught my attention and I asked him to tell me about it. If this kid was willing to put everything on the line for his startup, it had to be something good. He smiled, stood a little taller, and responded: "It's Tinder," he grinned, "for dogs." It took me nearly fifteen minutes to persuade him that when a dog is in heat, man's best friend doesn't really need an app to find a suitable mate.

No matter how hard you work, you need to have a solid idea and a plan to back it up. That's the only way you're going to build a team, attract investment, win over initial clients, and find the nerve to actually get going. The idea doesn't have to be perfect—initial business plans rarely are—but it has to have promise.

An *Inc.* magazine poll found that 71 percent of founders hit upon the idea for their company based on problems they faced while at previous jobs.[12] That means that your best bet is to stay put and keep your head down until you find an idea that can justify all the risks, costs, stress, and rejection you'll face as you figure out if it will actually work. Once you have the right idea, you will focus all your time and energy on testing, validating, refining, and improving it. Until you get to that point, your only option is to bide your time. This is too important a decision for you to settle for something that's mediocre.

5. Failure Sucks

Every once in a while, I hear the kind of cautionary tale that sends shudders down the spine of anyone who has ever thought of pursuing entrepreneurship as a career. One of the more memorable stories concerns a guy I'll call "Mr. Unlucky," one of the stars of his class at a top business school. While the rest of his contemporaries headed for Wall Street, consulting firms, or high-powered corporate positions, he opted for the first of a string of failed startups. Fifteen years later, Mr. Unlucky created quite a buzz among his former classmates when he moved back in with his mother. He was financially devastated and, apart from the gilded name of his alma mater, he had nothing to show for his efforts, since the only companies on his resumé were failed and forgotten. Mr. Unlucky wasn't stupid and he didn't necessarily make bad decisions. In fact, given his intellect, his pedigree, and his network, he just as easily could have hit it big. But things hadn't worked out in his favor. So instead of starting his days looking out over the ocean from the deck of his yacht, he ate Cheerios across the kitchen table from his mom.

Common perceptions of entrepreneurship make the march toward becoming a millionaire, or even a billionaire, seem inevitable. Here's the dirty little secret: the odds are you're going to fail. Consider a recent study by Harvard Business School professor Shikhar Ghosh tracking the fate of more than two thousand startups.[13] Ghosh reports that roughly 75 percent of them did not deliver promised returns to investors, while 30 percent to 40 percent returned little to no capital at all.[14] His findings speak to a fundamental reality of entrepreneurship: failure, like it or not, is part of the DNA of building new companies. In some circles, it is even celebrated as a badge of honor, an essential building block of what will eventually be a successful outcome, if not at this company, then at the next one. As long as you take something from the experience, they say, the failures will become hazy memories when bathed in the sunny glow of success. Legendary venture capitalist Marc Andreessen has even coined the term "failure fetish" to describe the somewhat paradoxical exaltation of failure in entrepreneurial circles. Raising a lone voice against all those failure fanatics, Andreessen has gone on the record to say something that seems pretty obvious to me: he thinks failure "sucks."[15]

If your chances of failure are better than even, then what happens if the odds work against you? If you fail multiple times, can you continue to bear the associated financial, emotional, and social costs? At some point, the price of entrepreneurship starts to escalate. This reality is especially stark if you want to get married, start a family, or buy a house. If you haven't yet "made it," the implications are clear: failure sucks, and you may not be able to afford it.

Entrepreneurship Is Not an All-or-Nothing Proposition

So now that I've given you five perfectly good reasons not to pursue *full-time* entrepreneurship, it's time to turn to the clear benefits that come with pursuing *part-time* entrepreneurship. In an ideal world, your job would provide you with an optimal mix of stability and upside—that would be the Holy Grail. There's only one problem. Like the Holy Grail, that kind of job is also impossible to find; people have been looking for both of them for the past two thousand years. That leaves you with a dilemma. If you're seeking upside, the conventional wisdom suggests that you should opt for entrepreneurship. The problem is that doing so entails considerable risks. Conventional wisdom also says that traditional career paths are supposed to maximize stability, even though that notion is increasingly a relic of the past. Faced with these stark alternatives, you are limited to two seemingly irreconcilable and suboptimal paths. You go one way or you go the other, accepting that each has definitive downsides.

Fortunately, the conventional wisdom is obsolete and you do not need to choose one course over the other. If you abandon the idea that one job is supposed to provide everything you need, you will see that traditional careers and entrepreneurship are not mutually exclusive. Instead, they can be complementary. Rather than choosing between a stable day job and entrepreneurship, why not allow your day job to provide the stability, the cash flow, and the platform to integrate entrepreneurial ventures into your career on the side? By expanding your career laterally rather than vertically, you can channel a meaningful percentage of your time and energy into something far broader. In this sense, entrepreneurship can enhance your career and serve as an avenue to generate upside as well as downside protection, all without requiring you to assume the risk of going all in.

Through part-time entrepreneurship, you will achieve more than just financial or professional diversification. You will embark on a series of adventures that will make your life richer and more interesting. The next time you're at a cocktail party or you run into an old friend on the street, you'll find yourself talking about the new startup or the real estate deal that you're working on rather than complaining about the slog at the office. By learning the ins and outs of entrepreneurship on your own time and on your own dime, you'll also gain a level of experience and credibility that you'd never find working for somebody else. With each opportunity you pursue, you will acquire skills that will allow you to bring renewed focus and vigor to your day job. In addition, everything you create for yourself will become part of your resumé and your investment portfolio, no matter what happens in your day job.

As you will see in the next chapter, engaging in entrepreneurship on the side will grant you a level of freedom that you could never access as a full-time entrepreneur. You will be able to partake in the excitement that comes from building something new while avoiding the stresses that come with taking risks. You can experiment with ideas that you might want to pursue full time, but you can do so without putting all your eggs in one basket or jeopardizing your lifestyle. Instead, you can employ a sustainable, pragmatic strategy that will complement and diversify your existing career. After all, your life, like your investment portfolio, is best when it's diversified.

Chapter 2

All the Benefits Without the Pitfalls

When Alex Torrenegra immigrated to the United States from Colombia at the age of eighteen, he spoke little English and could only find a job working the graveyard shift at McDonald's. Although he was a gifted programmer who founded his first company at the tender age of fourteen, he started out at the bottom in his adopted country. After seven months, he inched closer to the world of technology—trading cleaning toilets and flipping burgers for selling PlayStations as assistant manager of a video game store. Once he improved his English, he made the leap to a programming job. Not long after, Alex met Tania Zapata. Like Alex, she had also emigrated from Colombia, initially finding work as a receptionist at a Miami radio station. In between manning the phones, she filled in on the radio and began building her resumé as a voice-over artist.

When Alex met Tania, he didn't just meet his future wife, he also met his business partner. Even as they held down ordinary day jobs, they built what would eventually become Bunny Inc., the world's leading marketplace for voice-over artists. Tania understood the artists, their clients, and the industry's competitive dynamics, while Alex brought the technical skills needed to drive the entire industry online. A decade later, thousands of talented people now lend their voices to movies, commercials, video games, and electronic devices through Bunny Inc.'s online platform. From their headquarters in San Francisco, Alex and Tania manage an international team of more than fifty employees, forty of whom are based in Bogotá, Colombia. Given his success, Alex has been recognized by the White House and met with President Obama as part of the campaign for immigration reform.

It's easy to forget that Alex and Tania faced long odds when they dreamed of starting a company. They overcame multiple barriers, ranging from cultural and linguistic to professional. Unlike many of their peers in Silicon Valley, they didn't have the network or the credibility to put together a business plan and raise capital to get started. They also didn't have the savings to quit their jobs and dive in headfirst. As a result, they took the only path that was available to them: they became part-time entrepreneurs. Taking an incremental approach allowed them to test their ideas while keeping costs and risks at a minimum. They were also able to build something together, having fun in the process and creating a business that now offers them a level of upside and impact that could never have been possible in their previous careers.

As Alex and Tania demonstrate, pursuing entrepreneurship on the side offers several clear advantages that come without the risks of diving into the deep end of the pool. This chapter will lay out the four benefits of pursuing part-time, rather than full-time, entrepreneurship. First, you give yourself downside protection and diversification in the form of a Plan B that lessens the blow of unexpected career challenges. Second, you unlock sources of upside. As the old adage goes, nothing ventured, nothing gained; becoming an owner gives you the opportunity to create real value by taking part in promising new ventures. Third, diversification has a side effect that goes far beyond the potential economic benefits—it makes life more engaging and interesting. Finally, by embarking on a series of entrepreneurial journeys, you develop a set of critical skills that will make you a more complete professional. You will be able to draw upon everything you learn in your 10% to make a greater impact at your day job.

Plan B

If you go to any college campus, sit in the back of Finance 101, and listen in on the first day of class, you'll hear the professor ask her students the following question: What is the trick to successful investing? The answer is clear: diversification. When you're coming up with an investment strategy, you must design and build a portfolio that will weather good times and bad. If you're properly diversified, you minimize the risk that one failed investment will materially impact your wealth. Ironically, most of us do exactly the opposite with our careers. If you think of your career as an investment, and of course it is, then your portfolio, and by extension your life, is heavily exposed to just one position: your job. That's too much risk to bear, so you must find a way to make diversification a nonnegotiable part of your game plan. If you're looking for downside protection, you need a Plan B.

No matter what they do for a living, nearly every one of my friends has gone through a major career "adjustment" (that's the charitable word for "meltdown") since we graduated from college.

Most have found themselves out of work, longing to change jobs, or simply unhappy and lost. In the space of a year or two, I've seen people go from hero to zero with very little warning. That's the flip side of the opportunities for economic advancement that come with capitalism. You can do everything right and it doesn't make a difference. Even if you survive one financial crisis, there's sure to be another. Anything can happen, whether it's a restructuring, a merger, or any of the other sweeping changes that can cost you your livelihood.

Josh Newman learned the value of downside protection early in his career. His first job out of college was at Connecticut-based Modem Media, then one of the world's largest interactive advertising agencies. Those were the go-go days of the late 1990s Internet boom, and as a Web designer and developer, his skills were in high demand. When he discovered that Modem charged its clients an hourly rate that was around ten times what they paid him, he got an idea. Why not establish a boutique agency to provide the same kinds of services to much smaller clients that couldn't afford to work with a big agency? On nights and weekends, he launched a small firm called Mediatavern and built up a roster of clients. This presented no issues with his superiors at Modem Media since he always put his day job first and never competed for business.

When the tech bubble burst and he lost his job, Josh packed up his office and decided to see what he could make of Mediatavern. Having an alternate source of income meant that he didn't worry about paying the rent while looking for employment. It also made it easier for him to evaluate job offers as they came his way, since he knew how much he could earn on his own. In the end, he never found a job that was more attractive than putting all his energies into Mediatavern.

Since deciding to go all in, Josh built a company that now caters to Fortune 500 clients and is included in the *Inc.* 5000, a designation given to the fastest-growing firms in the United States. He's also never forgotten the mind-set that allowed him to thrive in the face of a career challenge. He runs Mediatavern like a true 10% Entrepreneur, dedicating a portion of the company's time and profits to developing and spinning off new businesses. He also partnered with his wife, Lisa, to create a new boutique digital agency catering to the small clients that got him started in the first place.

As Josh learned firsthand, there's no room for complacency when managing your career, so you need a Plan B. Your career will be affected by myriad events that are completely beyond your control, so you need to find a way to stay resilient. You will live through recessions, management shuffles, strategic shifts, and changes in priorities, all of which are out of your hands. If you set yourself on a path that includes built-in downside protection, the next time you face uncertainty, and it's very likely going to happen sooner than you think, you'll be ready. It's still not going to be a picnic, but you'll feel more secure knowing you have a backup plan.

Upside Opportunity

At its core, entrepreneurship is about being an owner. You can work for years collecting paycheck after paycheck, but if you're not an owner, the opportunity to build real wealth is usually limited. When I was just starting in the investment business, one of my colleagues sat me down and explained that as an employee of the firm, I would own a tiny piece of each of its investments.

He looked at me with gravity and said, "Patrick, that is the gift that keeps giving." I wasn't quite sure what he meant. Other than a bunch of clothes and gadgets, I'd never really owned anything before, certainly not part of a company. What were the benefits? "The thing is," he continued, "even if you leave this place, you'll be getting checks in the mail for the next five or ten years." That's the value of ownership. Once you own something, it's yours forever and it will benefit you in unexpected ways.

As a 10% Entrepreneur, you can create a portfolio of economic activities that will represent the "gift that keeps giving" for you. In doing so, you will accumulate economic interests in ventures or projects that have the potential to generate an attractive return on investment over time. Bear in mind that this is a long-term strategy, not a get-rich-quick scheme. Sure, you may have an investment or two that result in significant returns over a short period, but that isn't the norm. Your goal is to do the things that you enjoy in order to build real value over the long run. Whether you realize upside by investing your time or your energy, you can unlock multiple pathways to real financial returns.

Take the case of Bunny Inc. When I met Alex a few years ago, he asked me to join the company as an Advisor. As you'll see in the next chapter, Advisors commit their time, or sweat equity, to a company and are compensated with shares of its stock. The deal is simple. In exchange for working with senior management for two hours per month over two years, the company granted me 0.5 percent of its stock. My relationship with Bunny Inc., is based on the CEO's confidence that I can provide ongoing help with strategy, advice, and introductions. While the agreed time commitment fits within my 10%, the company also benefits from all the knowledge, connections, and insights I develop in the other 90% of my professional life. It's a symbiotic arrangement that is rewarding, both personally and financially.

Whether you're investing your time or your money, becoming an owner gives you access to a universe of upside opportunities that you'll never get if you don't have a piece of the action. So what does this mean in dollars and cents? If you believe the *Economist*'s valuation of the company, then today my shares are worth around $250,000, with plenty of room to grow in value.[1] That's a pretty nice return on my investment of time and energy, especially if you break it down on an hourly basis.

Make Life Richer and More Interesting

If you're thinking about becoming a 10% Entrepreneur, the chances are good that you've said one or more of the following to yourself:

"I like my job, but somehow, I expected more. I mean, I'm exactly where I always wanted to be and sort of think to myself . . . is this it?"

Or:

"I've always wanted to have a business of my own, but there's no way I can afford to leave the firm at this point. It would be crazy to walk away from a good situation, but I don't want to give up on my dream entirely. I need a way to enjoy the best of both worlds."

Or:

"I miss working with entrepreneurs and launching something new. I feel like I'm at my best when I'm outside of my comfort zone, but I'm not looking to venture completely out of my comfort zone."

Or:

"I know all kinds of people and I seem to be helping them do this kind of stuff anyway, but for free. There's got to be a way to monetize all those connections."

Or even:

"I'm basically checked out at work, but I can't afford to leave. I don't want to look back someday with regret, but I'm not sure how to get out of this rut."

There's a common theme in all these messages: We want more. We want to connect with new people, try new ideas, monetize our networks and knowledge, collaborate to solve problems, and be part of something that is bigger than ourselves. Most important, we want to continue to learn and grow both as professionals and as people. Each and every investment I have made in my portfolio of side ventures has generated returns that go well beyond dollars and cents. I've met terrific people, developed valuable skills, and contributed as much as I could to making each of these endeavors more successful than if I weren't in the picture.

Financial planning firms like to produce advertisements that tout the benefits of carefully preparing for retirement. If you pay attention, you'll notice that these commercials typically feature some smiling retiree who is finally packing it in, happy in the knowledge that he's saved wisely and can now do whatever he wishes. Every time I see one of those ads, I'm struck by the fact that they are hopelessly out of date. Who wants to wait until they're retired to pursue their dreams? Why does working on projects of your choosing have to come after your career? Why can't you do these things alongside everything else and then keep doing them even after you "retire"?

Dan Gertsacov isn't going to wait for retirement to do the

things he loves. A native of Rhode Island, he now lives in Bogotá, Colombia, where he's the chief digital officer at Arcos Dorados (McDonald's Latin America). Given Dan's general zest for life, as well as his experience opening Google's Colombia office, it's not too surprising that he's a 10% Entrepreneur. He's invested in or advised a number of companies in the technology, publishing, and e-commerce spaces in Latin America. I've even had the chance to see him in action since we're both Advisors at Bunny Inc.

Although he's got a full plate with his job at McDonald's (no pun intended), his side projects, and his family, Dan makes time to sharpen his skills as a chef, and his vacations often include multiple days at cooking schools. Having studied at various culinary academies, Dan already knew that he didn't want to be a chef. It was a terrific way to unwind during his free time and over vacations, but it was not how he wanted to spend all of his days. So he found another way to integrate this passion into the rest of his life—by pursuing it on the side and investing in La Xarcuteria, a local restaurant run by a promising chef. Not only did it offer financial upside for him, it enriched his life profoundly.

Ask any parent, and he or she will tell you that they want their children to be well rounded. Why then, do we abandon that principle for ourselves as adults? Perhaps you love to build furniture, you're a weekend photographer, or you're an interior design enthusiast. If money were no object, you'd pursue that discipline as a career, but you also recognize that absent financial independence, you'd face heavy trade-offs. It's natural to opt for security over passion, since very few people are willing to make the corresponding financial and personal sacrifices to do the opposite. That doesn't mean you have to settle. Rather than dabbling here and there or simply putting off doing the things you enjoy until you reach retirement, you can pursue part-time entrepreneurial ventures that integrate your personal interests and allow you to practice them in a meaningful, professional, and profitable way.

Build a Stronger and More Entrepreneurial Career

On the surface, engaging in ventures outside of your day job is rooted in self-interest. You are using your skills, your network, and your knowledge, some of which you acquired at your full-time job, to create more opportunities for yourself. At the same time, by taking on this challenge and focusing on yourself, you are developing and deepening a series of skills and relationships and flexing a different set of muscles that will make you more effective at the office.

Most any business you can think of is looking for ways to spur entrepreneurship within its ranks. In a time of rapid change, companies are hungry for fresh thinking and creative leadership that can steward them into the next stage of growth. These skills are critical whether you are a manager at a small manufacturing business in Michigan or a partner at Goldman Sachs. Unfortunately, most companies struggle to teach these kinds of competencies within a corporate environment. No matter how many training courses or exercises you complete, the only way to learn how to think like an entrepreneur is to do it.

If companies want to do more than just talk about innovation, they need to find a better way to foster a culture that teaches entrepreneurship. Some companies, even seemingly staid and traditional corporations, actively ask their workers to think beyond their job descriptions. In a sense, they're developing their own 10% Entrepreneurs as a way to drive creative thinking and discover the next great ideas. The Post-it was an outcome of

3M's famed "bootlegging" policy, which encourages personnel to spend up to 15 percent of their work time on their own projects. More recently, Google pioneered its renowned 70-20-10 model by asking their employees to allocate a portion of their time to projects outside the core business. Both these companies, and many others, could take things to the next level and become leaner, faster, and more innovative by encouraging their people to unleash their entrepreneurial talents outside of the office, and then find ways to channel those experiences back at work.

Hillyer Jennings's entrepreneurial activities have directly benefited his work as an attorney. A University of Georgia fan in the extreme (his kitchen is decorated with the school's official colors), he is also the creator of Wrist Tunes, which makes brightly colored music bracelets outfitted with speakers that play a clip of a song. If you're a Georgia fan, that means you can play the Bulldogs' fight song, "Glory, Glory," for everyone to hear, whether you're at a Georgia football game or at Machu Picchu, as Hillyer demonstrates on the company's Web site.

Sounds pretty fun, right? It's also a real business. After Hillyer started the company while in law school, Wrist Tunes raised capital from investors, licensed the UGA logo and fight song, applied for two patents, and secured a manufacturing partner in Asia. Through his Web site and a distribution network of more than a hundred stores, Hillyer has sold nearly $50,000 worth of bracelets . . . so far. Those are just the sales from one university. Now that he's validated the business model, imagine what Wrist Tunes can achieve when it targets other large alumni communities. Moreover, Hillyer can manage the business, experiment with new product extensions, and explore opportunities for growth, all while building his resumé as a corporate lawyer.

When you choose entrepreneurship, you take risks, build new contacts, and become a more versatile professional. You also learn how to sell yourself and better understand how you can add value to a business. None of these activities has to take away from your day job; in fact, they can be highly symbiotic. Hillyer is convinced that Wrist Tunes has real potential, but he's also very happy to keep his day job. He values the challenges, learning opportunities, credibility, and financial stability that come with working at a law firm. At the same time, Wrist Tunes has given him a series of experiences that make him a far more commercially minded lawyer. Having run his own business, he sees the world differently, more in line with his clients' views, than he would have otherwise.

There's no need to hide or labor in the shadows. All the people you will meet in this book are open about their activities, precisely because they do not compromise their commitment to their full-time jobs. Instead, they're actually more effective because of them. Imagine if your company bought you a copy of this book and encouraged you to pursue projects in your free time. What would that say about its dedication to developing talent within its ranks? By supporting you while you build a part of your career for yourself, your company would be making something very clear: it wants to attract and retain the best people possible.

You Can Tailor Entrepreneurship to Your Life as Never Before

Every idea or project begins with an impulse. What if I invested in that company? What if I tried to start a little side business? A light goes on in your head, you get inspired, and you permit yourself to dream. That's the honeymoon phase. It's fun, but you haven't yet kicked the tires or faced any resistance. These impulses are an essential part of any entrepreneur's journey, but they are only the beginning of a much larger endeavor.

The good news is that there has never been a better time to launch and manage an entrepreneurial venture. We live in a connected and highly mobile world in which technology is ubiquitous and inexpensive. As a result, for the first time in history you can work on whatever you want at the time and location of your choosing. As long as you've got an Internet connection, a smartphone, and perhaps a laptop, you're in business. Whether you decide to open a shop on Etsy, set up an e-commerce Web site for Wrist Tunes, or perform voice-overs at Bunny Inc., you can sell goods and services to clients all over the world from wherever you want.

It all comes down to flexibility. Flexibility enables you to keep costs down, stay nimble, and work in whatever manner makes the most sense for you. You know all those people you see with laptops when you go to your local coffee shop? The ones who make you ask yourself "Why is everyone on vacation but me?" They are probably not on vacation—they are the new mobile worker. You can be sitting at a café in London, Seoul, or Cape Town, but as long as you're connected, you're fully operational. Once you're up and running, you can manage your costs and stay nimble thanks to the sharing economy. If you decide you want an office, companies like WeWork provide on-demand office space in cities across the globe. Labor is also increasingly flexible and on demand. Thanks to people like Alex and Tania at Bunny Inc., as well as online work platforms like Upwork,[2] you can build your Web site, design your logo, draw up blueprints, or record your next radio commercial by working with freelancers from all over the world.

All these trends are your friends. They create the conditions that make part-time entrepreneurship far more accessible than ever. They also allow you to tailor entrepreneurship to the rest of your life. As you will see in the next chapter, just as there is no one type of entrepreneur, there is no one type of 10% Entrepreneur. Depending on your background and your interests, you can contribute a variety of resources, such as time or money, to each endeavor. In exchange for that contribution, you will create options that will offer you some or all of the advantages discussed in this chapter. They are the *why* of becoming a 10% Entrepreneur, and you might very well choose more than one path in order to fulfill multiple objectives.

Chapter 3

The Five Types of 10% Entrepreneurs

When he was growing up, entreprencurship never really factored into Peter Barlow's thinking. For a middle-class kid from Texas, medicine and law were both one-way tickets to an interesting, respectable, and comfortable life, and that's what he wanted. Law won out, but after a few years working at a firm, Peter jumped to a fast-growing software business, in search of a new challenge. Then, after discovering improprieties at the highest level of the company, he looked for an escape route. Having been burned, he developed a new-found appreciation for his old law firm, so he rejoined it, happily working in its aviation practice. It was a natural fit. From his grandfather on down, everyone in his family was obsessed with airplanes.

Back at the firm, Peter still kept an eye out for side ventures. Soon enough, a colleague from the misadventure at the software company invited him to help launch a luxury-auto brokerage. Since he loved cars just as much as he loved planes, Peter lent a hand during his free time in exchange for equity. The business grew steadily and it enabled him to broker sweet rides for himself and his partners at the law firm, all while keeping his day job.

At this point, he made another fateful plunge into entrepreneurship. His client Skybus Airlines was launching the first ultralow-cost carrier in the United States. Peter accepted the role of general counsel, convinced that this time all the pieces were in place. The company had a stellar management team and raised more than $150 million. What could go wrong? Unfortunately, the timing couldn't have been worse—Skybus launched just before the dual challenges of the 2008 financial crisis and a surge in fuel prices. In a matter of months, the company was no longer viable, and Peter worked with the executive team on the grim task of firing more than six hundred employees in the course of one afternoon. He returned to his law firm, this time for good. He'd lived through one failed venture too many, so if he was ever going to be an entrepreneur again, he would do so on the side.

He got his chance a year later when he noticed that the man sitting next to him on a plane was leafing through a pitch deck. It turned out that his seatmate, Todd Belveal, had spent the good part of two years working on a plan for an innovative car rental company. By the end of the flight, Peter was hooked on the idea and was convinced that he could help: he was a transportation attorney, he loved cars and planes, and he'd launched new ventures involving both. Peter and Todd exchanged information, and before long they were talking regularly to refine the pitch and the business model. Peter then called up Bill Diffenderffer, the former CEO of Skybus and a serial entrepreneur. After spending a weekend in front of a whiteboard hashing out the business plan, the three men agreed to become partners. Peter did so on the condition that he would stay at his law firm—from now on, he was going to be a 10% Entrepreneur.

Today, the company is known as Silvercar and it is renowned for completely reinventing the car rental experience. There are no lines or paperwork, and Silvercar's fleet consists entirely of silver Audi A4s. What was once only an idea in a pitch deck has now become a dynamic business. By the end of its third year of operations, the company managed a fleet of more than a thousand silver Audis at over ten locations across the United States. It also raised in excess of $50 million from investors, including Audi and Eduardo Saverin, the cofounder of Facebook. Now that he's the managing partner of his law firm's New York office, Peter Barlow doesn't have the bandwidth for any formal responsibilities at Silvercar, but he maintains a meaningful ownership stake and has invested in every round of financing.

As you'll see in this chapter, you don't have to choose a single path. Once you develop a set of entrepreneurial skills, you can tailor your portfolio of activities to your goals and the resources at your disposal. Even though Peter abandoned the roller coaster of full-time entrepreneurship, he became a serial 10% Entrepreneur. By spotting opportunities that build on his strengths and then drawing on his knowledge and his network to make things happen, he's been an Angel investor, an Advisor, and a partner in two successful businesses, all while maintaining a robust law practice. In doing so, he's created significant upside at these side ventures while enjoying the stability of a successful and lucrative legal career.

10% Entrepreneurship Is Not the Same as Freelancing

At this point, you might be asking yourself how being a 10% Entrepreneur differs from being a freelancer. Although freelancers integrate flexibility into the way they work, they are not 10% Entrepreneurs per se. Freelancers are contingent employees who charge a given rate for their time and are compensated with cash for their output. Some freelancers work with just one client. They are basically full-time employees without a long-term commitment. Others operate more like consulting firms that provide specialized resources by engaging in projects with multiple clients. Freelancers do not typically take ownership stakes in these projects or ventures, but rather focus on billing for services rendered.

As a 10% Entrepreneur, you will take a different approach. Since you already have a day job that provides you with steady income, you will use your 10% to build long-term value in various endeavors. You will think like an *owner* and use your time, your money, or a combination of the two to acquire or create equity stakes in one or more businesses. Put simply, you aren't billing by the hour. You're investing to become an owner.

If freelancing is as adventurous as you've been so far, there's no need to worry—it's a very natural first step on the road to 10% Entrepreneurship. As a freelancer, you will naturally have the opportunity to build a list of clients, expand your network, and assemble a track record of achievements that are your own. The name on your business card is yours and your work stands for itself. Now all you have to do is start thinking like an owner when the conditions permit. As you gain experience, you can actively seek out opportunities to partner with other entrepreneurs, trading your time and your expertise for sweat equity in exciting ventures that need and value your skills.

The Five Types of 10% Entrepreneurs

As you will see below, there are five types of 10% Entrepreneurs: Angels, Advisors, Founders, Aficionados, and 110% Entrepreneurs. As an Angel or an Advisor, you invest your capital, your skills, or both to help other people to grow their companies. Rather than starting companies yourself, you spend your time contributing to the success of ventures that are built and managed by others. In contrast, as a Founder, you create and manage your own businesses, even while you continue to hold down a day job. The last two types of 10% Entrepreneurs—Aficionados and 110% Entrepreneurs—represent a particular kind of Angel, Advisor, or Founder that pursues specific objectives: as an Aficionado, you are using entrepreneurship as a means of exploring your passions, while as a 110% Entrepreneur, you are already a full-time entrepreneur, so your primary goal is to diversify yourself.

1. The Angel

Venture capital firms may still rule Silicon Valley, but they are not the only game in town. That's where you come into the picture. At a time when it's only getting cheaper to start a company, lots of venture capitalists won't get out of bed to write small checks. That means that individuals like you and me are now an important source of financing for new ventures. These investors, called angel investors, were the first backers of companies like

Google, PayPal, Starbucks, and the Home Depot. In 2013, more than 300,000 angel investors funded some $24.1 billion into 73,400 companies,[1] representing an increase of approximately 60 percent over the last decade.[2]

Becoming an Angel is a logical first step to 10% Entrepreneurship for many people. It was for me. When I first started out, I wasn't yet sure how my new sideline would evolve, but I did know one thing—I wanted to get started. When I told friends and professional contacts of my aspirations, they began sharing investment opportunities with me. The types of companies and the capital required to invest varied widely, from $5,000 on up to $25,000 and sometimes more. It was my job to figure out how much money I wanted to commit to a given venture and then determine whether that venture had merit.

Farah Khan is an Angel who spends her days working at an investment firm that backs fast-growing companies in the consumer space. It's a role that keeps her busy, but where her firm's rules permit, she still makes time to invest her own capital in smaller companies that fall below her firm's minimum investment size. Farah sees a clear and mutually beneficial relationship between her day job and her personal investments. Early in her career, she realized that all the hours and effort she dedicated to managing investments for her employer taught her how those businesses actually worked. She learned what it takes to grow those companies from good ideas to industry leaders. It was an education and she paid attention.

For Farah, investing in ventures on the side isn't solely about building a portfolio of personal holdings that will make her money in the long run. It's also a way to up her game and benefit her firm at the same time. She keeps on top of industry trends and meets with talented entrepreneurs who are starting the next wave of exciting consumer-focused companies. That knowledge and those relationships inform her work at her day job and make her a better investor. When she meets entrepreneurs who run companies large and small, she can talk credibly from the perspective of someone who has helped to build businesses from the ground up.

As you can see, becoming an Angel has a clear financial dimension. So how much money do you need to commit? As with many questions in life, it depends. There are no written requirements or hard-and-fast rules about how much you *need* to invest, so it's really up to you and the founders of the company who are looking for capital. Angels typically participate alongside other early-stage investors, so you're only expected to contribute a portion of the capital raised. That said, if a company is raising $1 million, your $5,000 contribution probably won't get them too excited, unless you bring other nonfinancial assets to the table. On the other hand, if a company is raising a smaller amount of capital, $5,000 can be meaningful. In addition, you can always make your money count for more by banding together with other small investors or by joining an angel investment group. On the other end of the spectrum, some opportunities will require you to invest larger amounts of money, say $25,000 or more. Those may be appropriate for you, but as you'll see later, your capacity to invest will depend on how much money you determine you can allocate to your 10%.

When I first started as an Angel, I felt pretty insecure about the amount of capital I could invest. I wasn't the richest guy in the room and I didn't want to look poor or cheap compared to everyone else. Then I heard the story of Dick Costolo's investment in Twitter. When Twitter was raising money, its cofounder Evan Williams e-mailed Costolo, who'd just sold his company to Google, to ask whether he wanted to invest $25,000 or $100,000.

Costolo, who later went on to become Twitter's CEO, responded minutes later: "I'm on the $25k bus." His response completely changed my perception. If a guy who sold his company to Google feels comfortable being one of the smaller investors in a company, you can, too. Even "small" investments can pay off big: Costolo made millions by riding the 25k bus. You can make plenty of money by riding the 5k or 10k bus as well.

Investing in entrepreneurial ventures, either on your own or as part of a group, isn't just about upside, it's also about fun. You can dive into the challenges that small and fast-growing businesses encounter almost continually. You can also apply the knowledge that you've developed over the course of your career for your own benefit. If you've been working in a given sector and know it like the back of your hand, becoming an Angel can help you to monetize that knowledge while allowing you to build a network of entrepreneurs and investors who will be your partners in other projects. Finally, investments can provide on-ramps to other roles. On some occasions, you might be able to earn sweat equity alongside your cash investment, thereby increasing your overall returns without putting more principal at risk. As a 10% Entrepreneur, you don't necessarily have to contribute cash to become a shareholder in a company.

2. The Advisor

Maybe you have more to offer in the form of experience than in cash. In that case, you can serve as an Advisor. When you're an Advisor, you don't invest capital—your currency is your expertise. New companies, especially when they are first starting out, cannot afford to hire all the people they need to push their business forward. Instead, they work with a small team, one on which everyone is required to be a jack-of-all-trades. Only later, as the business scales, will the various functions solidify into departments such as marketing, operations, finance, and sales. Until that time, companies need to multitask. Everyone from the CEO on down takes on several roles and responsibilities, often working in areas where they lack deep experience. As an Advisor, you can help to fill gaps in knowledge until a startup is ready to hire full-time talent. You can also provide the credibility and perspective of someone who's "been around the block."

It's safe to say that in the e-commerce world, Beth Ferreira's experience classifies her as having been around the block. She started her career as a venture capitalist and management consultant before becoming vice president of operations and finance at Etsy, and later taking on the chief operating officer role at Fab.com. While at Fab, she built and managed an operation that shipped 250,000 packages per month and grew the company's warehouse staff from 0 to 250 employees. Because of her considerable operational credibility, she's in high demand. She's been an Advisor to companies like Birchbox, Pixable, and Coupang, a South Korean e-commerce site that raised more than $1 billion in capital. When these companies call her, they aren't looking for cash. They are looking for help. As Beth puts it, "Someone who is writing a check usually didn't sit in a warehouse for two years understanding how to make things function."

So how does all this work? As an Advisor, you commit to a certain number of hours per month and are compensated in the form of stock. While the advice or expertise you provide can be general in nature, depending on your talents you might help with anything from making key introductions to creating a set of financial projections, reviewing a lease, designing a logo, or preparing marketing or fund-raising materials. Although compensation varies, most Advisors receive anywhere from .2 percent to 2 percent of a company and typically set aside a few hours a month for a period of a year of more. You can also work on a short-term basis on one-off projects.

You don't need to be a hacker or a marketing whiz to score Advisor equity. Take the case of David Choe. Choe is the graffiti artist who took stock in Facebook as payment for murals he painted at their headquarters. When Facebook went public, his shares, which likely accounted for less than .25 percent of the company when they were awarded, were valued at hundreds of millions of dollars.[3] When you compare the thousands of dollars he would have received in cash to the fortune he received in stock, it's clear that holding even a tiny slice of equity in the right company can change your life.

Beyond earning equity, you'll enjoy other benefits as well. First, you can use your Advisor roles to learn new skills, tackle interesting challenges, and deepen your knowledge of an industry. Second, you can expand your network to include lots of talented entrepreneurs, some of whom might become real players in their industries. Third, you often have the option of becoming an Angel when the company raises money. Finally, Advisor positions become natural on-ramps to larger, even full-time, roles if a company really takes off. If you work well with the team, you might decide to join them in that capacity. From Beth's perspective, you never know where being an Advisor might take you, so it's a good chance to "try before you buy."

3. The Founder

It's a cold January day and I find myself sitting at a waterfront restaurant wondering what to order. "Get the lobster bisque,"

Luke suggests. I nod and follow his lead. I'm not going to dis-agree with a guy who sells millions of dollars of lobster rolls at eponymous restaurants up and down the East Coast. Luke Holden is the Founder of Luke's Lobster. He's also "Mr. Lobster" around these parts. That really means something when "these parts" refers to Portland, a cozy city set along the coast of Maine and the world's lobster capital. He sits on the board of direc-tors of the Lobster Institute and he's been named to "30 Under 30" lists by *Inc.*, *Forbes*, and Zagat. Not bad for someone who hatched the idea for his lobster business and oversaw much of its first year of operations while working full time in corporate America.

As a Founder, you seek to balance the best of both worlds by maintaining full-time employment even as you launch entrepre-neurial ventures. By doing so, you can create options beyond your day job, but without risking the stability, prestige, and fi-nancial rewards that come from steady employment. This gives you the chance to determine whether a venture is viable and whether you enjoy leading an enterprise. If the new business gains traction and requires more time than you can give, then you have a decision to make: do you leave your day job and be-come a full-time entrepreneur, or do you maintain the status quo, stick to your day job, and find a partner who can help you take things to the next level?

I first heard about Luke's Lobster because like any New Yorker who hails from the state of Maine, I wanted to find a good lob-ster roll. Back home, we'd all grown up eating lobster rolls off paper plates while seated at picnic tables. Somehow, New York chefs had decided that lobster was a white tablecloth experience. Their pricing reflected that bias. I was lucky that Luke Holden, who also comes from Maine, had faced that same quandary. One day, after a few years working up to ninety hours a week at an investment bank, he decided to do something about it. Luke's simple yet ingenious plan was to bring the rituals he knew from back home to the masses of Manhattan, thus transforming lobster from a once-a-year splurge into an affordable luxury.

Luke didn't start his company because he wanted to escape the rigors of Wall Street to become America's lobster czar. Although he was excited about his idea, he originally had no intention of leaving his day job. He liked the intellectual challenge, respected his colleagues, and knew that the training and experience it provided would be indispensable for whatever he did next. He also needed the money. When Luke first moved to New York, he had nothing to his name but a pile of credit-card debt. Now, after working for a few years, he had some savings, but he was not in a position to quit his job. At this point, he faced a crossroads: he could find the time to develop a business plan or he could put his dreams on hold and pick them up again in the future. There was probably never going to be a perfect time to choose entrepreneurship in terms of his schedule or his finances, so he resolved to explore the business on the side, happy to have a steady job to pay the bills while he formulated a course of action.

After writing a business plan, Luke knew he needed help if he was going to work full time while opening his first stores. He found his business partner, Ben Conniff, on Craigslist and then scraped together $35,000 to open the first Luke's Lobster shop in a tiny East Village storefront. Within seventeen days he had recouped the entire cost of building out the store. Still, even with this early success, Luke continued to work in banking for nearly a year before taking a 75 percent pay cut to earn $35,000 a year as president of the company. Five years later, Luke's Lobster had some twenty stores in seven American cities and in Tokyo. Between the retail operations and his seafood processing plant in Maine, Luke employed more than 250 people.

Unlike an Angel or an Advisor, who endeavors to construct a portfolio of positions, as a Founder you will focus all of your attention on one company and you will have operational control. Together with Ben, Luke carries the fate of the business on his shoulders. This means that he assumes more risk than an Angel like Farah Khan or an Advisor like Beth Ferreira—he's less diversified—but it also means that he can potentially see much bigger returns. He owns a meaningful percentage of a company that's got millions in sales, a killer brand, and deeply loyal customers in multiple geographies. Plus, there's plenty of room to grow since Luke's Lobster has only scratched the surface of what is a large and attractive market. It's still not yet certain just how much his company will be worth as it expands, but it's clear that Luke owns a nice share of something that has huge promise. When you put it that way, it sounds like Farah should consider investing in Luke's Lobster.

As a Founder, you must strike a delicate balance between your day job and your other commitments. If you're running around building a business for yourself, how do you make sure that it doesn't conflict with or contaminate the work you're doing for others? In the digital age, it's hard to keep secrets. For Luke, the decision to be completely open with his employers about the lobster business was a no-brainer. First of all, his name was right there on the sign that hung over his shop on Seventh Street. Second, his firm's compliance group required him to report any meaningful personal business ownership. Whether your name is on a sign or not, you will want to respect your firm's policies. It's the right thing to do and it is also good business. Just ask Luke.

His colleagues at the bank were supportive of his ambitions and became some of his earliest and best customers.

4. The Aficionado

As an Aficionado, you channel meaningful time and energy, either as an Angel, an Advisor, or a Founder, into doing something you truly love. Even if you're engaging on a part-time basis, your interest is far from amateurish and you're not content with being a hobbyist. You don't want to play the trumpet alone in your garage and you're not satisfied with cooking elaborate dinners just for friends and family. Although you don't plan to pursue a favorite pastime as a career, you still aspire to apply your skills at the highest level possible, and you want to do so alongside professionals. This is an avocation, but one that you approach with the same level of professionalism as any Angel, Advisor, or Founder. The difference is that the driving motivation is passion rather than pure profit. Still, you will think like an entrepreneur so that your hard work can lead to a self-sustaining business opportunity.

When Mildred Yuan, my literary agent, first read the proposal for this book, I was surprised at how quickly she latched on to the concept. Then she told me that when she wasn't working at the agency, she was a professional dancer. She'd been dancing since she was a kid and even considered a career in dance. But as a self-described "child of Asian parents," she was discouraged from choosing a life in the arts, so she opted to study economics. With a career as a ballerina out of reach, she shifted her attention to ballroom dancing, since she'd enjoy greater longevity than in the ballet world. A few years later, she moved to London, the birthplace of ballroom dance, to join a strategy consulting firm and met Gary Crotaz, a new colleague who was also a dancer. They formed a partnership, first in dance and later in marriage, and dedicated their off-work hours to the London ballroom dance scene.

Mildred and Gary set clear priorities. Their relationship came first, then their careers, and then dance. Everything else—vacations, watching TV, sleep—was a secondary priority. The couple spent many vacations and at least one weekend per month training in Italy. If professional demands got in the way, they found ways to carve out a few precious hours to rehearse. When Mildred traveled to Abu Dhabi for a consulting assignment, Gary wrangled his own project there, and they rehearsed at 5 A.M., before it got too hot to continue. Although they made some sacrifices, the years of hard work, travel, and dedication paid off. They represented the United Kingdom in seven World and European championships and placed among the top eight pairs in the world. They also started a London-based academy to train the next generation of elite dancers.

Exploring another side of your talents can bring clarity to the rest of your career. You can build networks and acquire skills or insights that may even take you in an entirely new direction. The strategic thinking that Mildred employed every day as a consultant was in high demand among the dancers in her network, so she resolved to draw on both sides of her personality—the businessperson and the artist—by becoming an agent. In addition to writers, she now represents world champion dancers and leading choreographers, some of whom know her from the days when she danced competitively. Whether they danced with her or not, these clients appreciate the fact that she innately understands how they look at their craft. That sets Mildred apart in her field and gives her a competitive edge.

5. The 110% Entrepreneur

Once you open the entrepreneurial floodgates, it's hard to close them. If you've ever successfully started and managed a company, then you've moved to a point where launching something new is no longer intimidating. On the contrary, you see opportunities everywhere. You also accept the facts: the odds are against you. You are more likely to fail than to succeed, so you need to diversify yourself. After all, when you're working full time on an entrepreneurial venture, you are placing a very concentrated bet that will largely determine your future wealth. By making Angel investments or taking Advisor roles on the side, you can build a diversified portfolio of ownership stakes in ventures outside of your own startup, which offer downside protection while opening new doors. In that sense, you add your 10% to the 100% you are already allocating to entrepreneurship to become a 110% Entrepreneur.

Diego Saez-Gil is a textbook example of a 110% Entrepreneur. In 2011, he founded an online travel agency called WeHostels that specialized in backpackers and hostels. Two years later, when he merged the company with a student travel agency, he became the head of a division at the combined company. That should have been the end of the story. Except that it wasn't. Even though he realized that for the first time in memory he had a stable salary and a reasonable schedule, Diego also had a big idea. What if he set his sights on building the world's first piece of smart luggage? It would be an Internet-connected suitcase that travelers could track, lock, and weigh, all using a smartphone. He began talking with an entrepreneur who was also from Argentina, Tomi Pierucci, who had deep experience sourcing products from China. Tomi loved the idea and wanted to make it happen, so they agreed that he would take the lead. This time, Diego was going to be a 10% Entrepreneur, serving as an Advisor to Bluesmart and Tomi while keeping his day job.

When the company launched a crowdfunding campaign on Indiegogo in late 2014, the suitcase attracted enthusiastic media coverage and generated a lot of excitement. *USA Today* even called it "The travel hack to beat all travel hacks." By the end of its campaign, Bluesmart had sold more than $2 million worth of suitcases to customers in 110 countries. At the time, it was the seventeenth most successful campaign in Indiegogo's history, ranking in the top .006 percent of all projects based on money raised. After such a stunning campaign, the world took notice: Bluesmart joined Y Combinator, the legendary seed accelerator that spawned companies like Dropbox and Airbnb. It was also one of the first companies selected for Amazon Launchpad, which allows promising startups to market and sell their products through the Amazon platform.

When you make investments in your 10% you never know where they will take you. Given Bluesmart's stunning debut, Diego decided to once again become a 100% Entrepreneur, so he stepped up his involvement in Bluesmart and joined the company full time as CEO and cofounder. Since that time, the company has raised more than $10 million in funding. It's also part of my 10%—I'm both an Angel and an Advisor to Bluesmart, as well as one of their first satisfied customers.

What Are You Waiting For?

Whether you are well established or just starting your first job, you owe it to yourself to think about how your career will evolve over the course of the coming decades. It's impossible to know today how the labor market, and your role within it, will change. You will need to remain engaged, always looking for new opportunities and building new skills and relationships. That's the most effective way to make sure that you don't end up chasing yesterday's dream. It also represents a real commitment to building a career that is dynamic, resilient, and rewarding.

Yet even if lots of people, people like you, are becoming 10% Entrepreneurs, you might still wonder how to embrace entrepreneurship, even on a part-time basis, when you've never done so before. It's like there's a party going on and you're standing out in the cold, wondering why you didn't get an invitation. That's especially true if you never expected or even wanted to become an entrepreneur in the first place. Perhaps you played by an established set of rules that should have positioned you for prestige, success, and fulfillment. You invested countless hours following the perfect playbook without realizing that the game has changed or that you just want more. Careers, much like our lives, have arcs. They ebb and flow. There will be periods where you put your head down and work. There will be other times when you have more space to reflect, plan, and figure out your next move. You may very well look around one day and ask yourself "Is this it?" In that moment you realize that one job, no matter how much you like it, cannot give you everything you need.

Just because you've chosen a particular path doesn't mean you are complacent. As you look on from the sidelines, you see talented people flocking to industries where they can build careers that offer unprecedented levels of flexibility with respect to roles, location, and lifestyle. If you simply stick to the plan, you forgo the opportunity to get in on the action and partake in the upside. In the face of this quandary, you're left with one of two choices:

continue moving forward on cruise control, or start to make your own rules. Rather than letting your career happen to you, it's time to take the wheel, flip off cruise control, and hit the gas.

So what are you waiting for? If you find yourself standing on line and waiting for someone to let you into the party, then I have some good news for you. There's no reason you should be waiting outside in the cold. It's not too late and you can print your own ticket. You have something to offer, in the form of skills, knowledge, relationships, and wisdom, all of which are invaluable to entrepreneurial ventures. This is your currency to pay the price of entry, and it will allow you to orient your career in a way that offers far greater excitement and opportunity. Part 2 will provide you with everything you'll need to get started.

Part 2

Building Your 10%

Chapter 4

What Kind of 10% Entrepreneur Are You?

I n 2014, Atlanta's Monday Night Brewing sold 2.5 million bottles of beer to hundreds of thousands of customers. It's likely that most of those thirsty people never realized that they could literally thank God for the craft beers they held in their hands, but you could argue that there was at least a little divine intervention at play. The three Founders met at a 6 A.M. Friday morning Bible study. When they decided to spend Monday nights hanging out more casually, cofounder Joel Iverson remembered the home brewing kit languishing in his basement, so he suggested making beer. When their Monday night brewing sessions started attracting crowds of fifty people or more, Joel and his partners worked the taps and wondered: where are we going with all this?

A thousand miles away, the Founders of Oyster Bay Brewing Company manned the busy sales floor of a Long Island car dealership. Gabe Haim and Ryan Schlotter regularly brainstormed ideas for business ventures they could explore outside of their day jobs, until one night, over beers, they decided to order home brewing kits from Amazon. Their first batch wasn't half bad, so they brewed another, and another. As they got the hang of brewing for their family and friends, they noticed that there were no craft breweries anywhere in the vicinity of their homes. They, too, started to wonder: where are we going with all this?

It turns out that the beer industry is a natural home for a 10% Entrepreneur. Once you buy an inexpensive home brewing kit, you can work on your own schedule to learn the secrets of the trade, research the local market, and contact suppliers. The negligible cash required to get started means that there is little to lose beyond a commitment of time and energy. That's a game changer for someone like Joel Iverson of Monday Night Brewing. He developed infomercials for celebrities like Paula Abdul and even had a hand in marketing Hulk Hogan's Ultimate Grill (America thanks you, Joel), so he knew how to launch new products. Why not put his skills to the test for his own benefit?

Since starting a brewery out of a basement was a somewhat audacious idea, after two years of experimentation Joel and his partners decided it was finally time to answer that nagging question: where was the business going? They created a three-year plan and took a hard look at where they stood. Although they had mastered brewing small batches, they didn't have experience running a commercial brewery. Moreover, they wouldn't hit their growth targets without investing more in terms of time and money. With their challenges now clear, they got to work. First, they built relationships with everyone who could help them to succeed, from brewers to distributors. Next, they raised some working capital and launched their first beers by outsourcing production to a third party. Demand grew quickly, so they raised additional capital to build a brewery of their own. Eventually, two of the partners, including Joel, joined full time, and they recruited a first-rate brewmaster. Their plan worked: just three years after hitting the market, Monday Night Brewing generated millions in revenues and employed over sixty people.

For Gabe and Ryan, Oyster Bay Brewing Company remains a 10% investment. They like their day jobs and they appreciate the financial rewards that come with working at a successful auto dealership. In order to focus on their work there while still building their brewing empire, they hired a team to run Oyster Bay's day-to-day operations. They also relied on sweat and ingenuity to grow the business with minimal cash investment. Gabe and Ryan spent their free time renovating a defunct Mexican restaurant in a strip mall for their first brew pub. Thanks to a potent combination of social media marketing and strategic partnerships, they developed a strong brand and a rabid following on the North Shore of Long Island. Over time, their pluck and creativity paid off: Oyster Bay Brewing Company's beers were soon served at the stadiums of both the New York Islanders and the New York Mets, two of the most important sports franchises on the East Coast.

Entrepreneurship is about formulating a plan and then making choices, both big and small, that will help you to reach the next step of that plan. As an idea grows from a fun side project to a "what if," you'll tackle the very same questions as the teams from Monday Night Brewing and Oyster Bay Brewing Company. Where are you going? What will you need to get there? How much time and money can you invest? Once you have clear and honest answers to these questions, you will be equipped to set your course as a 10% Entrepreneur and make a 10% Plan. As you'll see in this chapter, although you'll never have perfect information and you can't predict the future, you can take steps today to be prepared. By assessing the resources you can bring to bear and then formulating a plan of action, you will be ready for each fork in the road.

Your Resources As a 10% Entrepreneur

As with any entrepreneur, you are going to make decisions with respect to your 10% based on your circumstances. You will stretch scarce resources, balance trade-offs, and then adjust accordingly. First, you will consider how much *time* you can dedicate to your efforts. Next, you will determine how much *financial capital*, or money, you can invest. Your aim is to set aside at least 10% of your resources in these areas, recognizing that these are targets and your capacity to invest will naturally evolve over time. Third, you will consider how *intellectual capital*, namely your base of knowledge and skills, fits into the picture. When it comes to intellectual capital, your goal is to combine the things you do well with the things you enjoy. Intellectual capital is the ingredient that will allow you to manage your investments of time and financial capital far more productively. Using your knowledge and your judgment, you will make smart, informed decisions that will, in turn, increase the likelihood of achieving successful outcomes.

Although each resource is discrete, when taken together, you can think of them like a portfolio. Each component is also dynamic, so your portfolio will change over time, depending on your stage in life, your financial resources, and your level of experience. As with any other investment portfolio, you will make calculated bets in order to grow the value of each individual asset while also maximizing their combined value. As your portfolio expands, you will broaden your range of options, enjoying greater flexibility with regard to how you deploy your resources, both separately and as a group. If you invest wisely, the return on these investments will compound, yielding far more than the sum of its parts.

The Resources of the 10% Entrepreneur

TIME   FINANCIAL   INTELLECTUAL
          CAPITAL   CAPITAL

Nobody has unlimited time, endless cash, or deep expertise in an infinite range of pursuits, but where you lack for one, you can often compensate by contributing more of another. By thinking of your resources as a portfolio, you can balance the areas in which you are lacking (perhaps capital) with the areas in which you have strength and abundance (such as time and know-how). When the Founders of Oyster Bay Brewing Company decided to keep their day jobs and fund the growth of the company themselves, the implications of these decisions were clear: they needed to invest both their time and their financial capital as efficiently as possible. Although it would have been easier and faster to hire a contractor to renovate the pub space, it would also have been far more expensive. They weighed their alternatives and opted to do the carpentry themselves, when they weren't selling cars, contributing time instead of financial capital in that instance.

At this point, you might be wondering what you should do if you cannot invest money. Is it possible to compensate by contributing time and intellectual capital instead of cash? It's a very good question, and one that lots of people ask themselves at this stage in the game. Always keep in mind that investing isn't just about money. New ventures need money, but they also need assistance from people like you who can offer a wide variety of skills and services. So even if you don't have financial capital, you can still invest in the form of sweat equity by using time and intellectual capital as your currency.

Depending on your skills, you will find abundant opportunities to work for sweat equity. There are plenty of services that young businesses will consider as an in-kind capital contribution in exchange for stock. Businesses also look for ongoing support such as legal advice, financial guidance, marketing expertise, or connections to business opportunities and partnerships. As they grow, they need help from people who come from lots of different backgrounds. Although none of these contributions are made in the form of cash per se, they are often just as valuable.

This approach is not limited to people who are unable to make cash investments. You may have plenty of capital to invest in new ventures, but that doesn't mean you're always going to want to be an Angel. Just because you enjoy working with early-stage ventures doesn't make you immune to risk. Perhaps you feel a company's risk profile is too high or its stage of development is too early for you to feel comfortable writing a check. Whether you have money to invest or not, becoming an Advisor, rather than an Angel, lets you take a seat at the table without putting money at risk. Even if you decide to invest as an Angel at some point, you can still consider taking an Advisor position to increase your upside in a particular investment. By doing so, you can make your money count for more.

How Resources Correspond to the Five Types of 10% Entrepreneurs

At this point, you might be tempted to dwell on the areas where you consider yourself lacking with respect to resources. Maybe you feel like you're too busy as it is, or you don't have financial capital to invest. Don't let that discourage you. You'll spend the next chapters thinking carefully about your resources and learning how to make the most of each of your assets. You'll also begin to craft a realistic strategy that is customized to your own particular circumstances. Before you actually dive into the details, however, it's worth thinking about how your resources will shape your options in a more general sense. As you'll see below, each distinct type of 10% Entrepreneurship draws on a particular combination of time, financial capital, and intellectual capital:

If You Want to Be an Angel . . .

If you're worried about time, becoming an Angel is a highly flexible form of engagement that works well if you're busy or have an unpredictable schedule. Entrepreneurs ideally seek out "smart money," meaning investors who can help them beyond investing cash alone, but your actual level of involvement is entirely determined by you. Depending on your interest in a particular project, you can foster relationships with the company, its management, and other investors. By doing so, you will learn more and build deeper connections that will benefit you in the future. You may also create an opportunity to take on a more formal role and increase your upside by becoming an Advisor. Everything you do after sending your check is optional, however, so if you don't have much time to get involved, there is no requirement to do so.

If you want to be an Angel but you aren't quite sure where to start, don't worry; you can supplement your intellectual capital with that of others. No matter if you are in Miami, Bucharest, or Beijing, as you'll see later, you can find other people who want to invest and work together. Joining an angel investment group will provide you with the resources and connections you'll need to find and invest in new ventures. It will also give you access to a community of like-minded people who will show you the ropes. According to the Angel Capital Association, there are more than three hundred such groups in the United States alone.[1] There are similar groups throughout Europe, Asia, and Latin America. You can usually find angels just about anywhere you find entrepreneurs. In fact, the farther you get from the places where venture capital firms typically operate, the more your capital and expertise will matter.

If You Want to Be an Advisor . . .

If you have more intellectual capital and time than money, you should consider becoming an Advisor. Since you are investing intellectual rather than financial capital, you must be able to dedicate a mutually agreed-upon amount of time to work with the companies that compensate you with equity. In practice, the expected investment of time can range significantly. Some companies are looking for steady advice, say an hour or two a month. They'll call you or meet with you to ask you for strategic ideas or connections, or just to brainstorm. That's my arrangement with

Bunny Inc. I commit to a minimum of two hours per month with the CEO and the VP of Finance, and then we jointly determine how I can help the company during the rest of the month. It's not much more time intensive than that, but I leave each of our conversations with a to-do list and we keep in touch via e-mail between meetings. Given this manageable investment of time, it's not uncommon for experienced Advisors like Beth Ferreira to work with a number of companies at the same time, all the while accumulating a portfolio of equity positions.

Many Advisors first get involved with companies that are still in the idea phase of their development. They are there in the early days to lend some credibility and support so that when the company goes out to raise money, it's able to show the world that it has serious people on its side. In such a case, you might consider requesting a right to invest when the company raises capital. In this way, acting as an Advisor is an on-ramp to becoming an Angel. Given your involvement, you're well placed to know whether the company is positioned for success, so you can generate additional returns based on all the things you have learned.

If You Want to Be a Founder . . .

As a Founder, you must be prepared to bring all of your resources to bear. If you're going to start a company, you need to carve out time to research the market, build key relationships, develop the product, and launch your business. All these tasks will draw upon the intellectual capital you've acquired over the course of your life. Although many of the basic tools of modern business are relatively inexpensive, there will be some ongoing costs, especially once you get going, so you may also end up investing some financial capital to cover basic expenses.

In your early days as a Founder, you may decide to operate on your own. That approach can work well, especially if the time commitment is manageable and the capital requirements are small. At some point, however, the demands on your schedule or on your wallet will increase. Depending on the type of business in question, you may need to develop a prototype, build inventory, sign a lease, or hire employees. You can then determine the most effective manner to marshal the additional resources you'll require to continue executing your business plan.

When faced with resource constraints, Luke Holden recruited a partner who had the intellectual capital and the time to commit to the daily operations of the business. He also approached his father, who co-invested with him to fund the cost of the initial Luke's Lobster store. In contrast, while Hillyer Jennings raised some capital from investors, he continues to run Wrist Tunes by himself with some help from his brothers. He supplemented his intellectual capital by outsourcing design and manufacturing to partners located in China.

If You Want to Be an Aficionado or a 110% Entrepreneur . . .

As an Aficionado or a 110% Entrepreneur, you can structure your involvement as you see fit and you can take an Angel, Advisor, or Founder role. You can also combine multiple roles as you tailor your investment to your resources. For example, Diego Saez-Gil is both an Advisor and a Founder at Bluesmart, while Dan Gertsacov is both an Angel and an Advisor to his restaurant. Each of them chose a strategy that reflected his overall objectives as well as his resources.

Charting a Course to Entrepreneurship: The 10% Plan

A couple of years ago, in the middle of winter, I hiked some remote stretches of the Tian Shan Mountains on an expedition in Kyrgyzstan. If you're going on a high-altitude hike in cold weather, you accept that it's going to be chilly, but the temperatures in the Tian Shan range can feel otherworldly. It's the kind of place where you fire up the weather app on your phone to discover that it's -40°F outside. That's dangerously cold, so when you step onto the mountain, your only option is to get moving. You put one foot in front of the other, sinking into the untouched field of snow, until you find the summit. You soon discover that with each step you get warmer. Over time, you start to feel hot, so you peel off some layers and stuff them in your bag. When your blood is flowing, the only way to maintain that warmth is to press on. If you stop, the cold returns and you're exposed.

Once you've been on the mountain for a while, you've gone over a few ridges, and all traces of civilization fade, you realize that you're relying on three basic elements to get you back safely. First, there's your plan. You've got the basic gear and you've charted a course that will take you to the peak and back by the time the sun goes down. Second, you've got your will. Your gear will not drag you to the summit and then guide you back down again. You have to see a purpose in the undertaking. If you don't, the cold, the altitude, and the length of the journey will cause you to question why you ever signed up for this lunacy in the first place. Finally, you're relying on the other people hiking alongside you, who you hope are just as committed as you are. Knowing that you are all blazing a path together keeps you from slowing down or wanting to quit. It also stokes your competitive spirit and makes you travel just a little bit faster. Still, competition aside, you stick to the group. You're all going to the same place and you'll want someone at the summit to share the experience with you.

As a 10% Entrepreneur, your journey is going to be a lot like climbing a mountain. When you're trying something new and heading in an unfamiliar direction, you don't know exactly what it's going to be like once you set off. You're not going to be facing the elements in a literal sense, but you will be pushing yourself out of your comfort zone, sometimes putting yourself into new settings where you feel uncomfortable or unsure. It is at these moments that having a game plan is essential. Like a climber struggling against cold and fatigue, you will survey the landscape and then stick to your plan. It will serve as your compass and point the way forward.

Of course, you can always choose to get started without preparing much of anything. You can leave the map at home, throw on a pair of hiking boots, and just walk out into the wilderness. That's how many people get going, almost by accident, by dipping a toe and taking a little risk. Still, it's an approach that I don't recommend. You will not have taken an honest look at your resources to see what kinds of investments are right for you, so you'll risk making decisions based on momentum or opportunism. More important, you'll miss the chance to chart a sustainable course and then execute it. The better your plan, the more likely it is that you'll make shrewd and profitable investments. With success, you will have even more options as you generate profits from your investments, reinvest those gains, and grow your base of resources to create a self-sustaining endeavor.

Your 10% Plan, which will serve as the blueprint for all of your efforts, draws upon two other important assets in addition to your resources. First, you will follow a well-defined *investment process* that will help you focus and make decisions with rigor. Following a standard procedure will allow you to deploy your resources wisely and to learn and improve as you go along. Second, you will mobilize your *network* to make everything tick. Drawing upon the combined resources of all the talented people you know will allow you to maximize the impact of the resources that you commit.

The 10% Plan

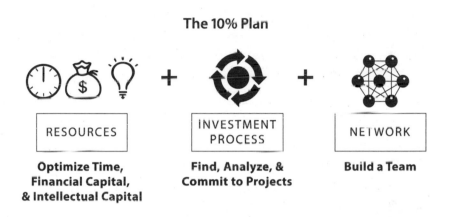

RESOURCES	INVESTMENT PROCESS	NETWORK
Optimize Time, Financial Capital, & Intellectual Capital	**Find, Analyze, & Commit to Projects**	**Build a Team**

If the idea of putting together a 10% Plan seems a bit daunting, consider this: you already got a head start by taking an initial look at how time, financial capital, and intellectual capital will shape your plan. Throughout the remainder of this book, you will take a closer look at each of these resources, plan your investment process, and begin to mobilize your network. I'll walk you through the process of assembling your 10% Plan along the way by helping you address the following questions:

- How much time and financial capital can you and will you commit to your 10%? *How will you make the most of time and money?*

- How can you find opportunities that pair the things you do well with your intellectual capital? *How will you draw upon your intellectual capital to play to your strengths?*
- How can you source relevant opportunities and then make informed investment decisions? *How will you apply your investment process to find, analyze, and commit to projects?*
- How can you mobilize your network to make each aspect of your 10% more successful? *How will you leverage your network to build your team?*

Your 10% Plan will be a living document that you will return to periodically. As you progress through each stage of planning, take notes, either electronically or in a notebook. These notes will serve as an ongoing resource to guide you, just like a compass and a map, as you chart a profitable course. Don't worry if your circumstances change; your 10% Plan is intended for the long term, so it's completely adaptable. If you get that bonus, move cities, develop new interests, or gain more flexibility in your schedule, you can return to your plan and adjust accordingly.

Chapter 5

Making the Most of Time and Money

When you become a 10% Entrepreneur, you never quite know where each opportunity will take you. I like to think of every project as if I'm planting a seed. Some seeds fail to germinate, some live and prosper, and others go on to produce new seeds that, after being scattered by the wind, set down roots in unexpected places. Over time, you will be able to chase after those seeds, taking part in one venture after another with a growing team of partners you know and trust from prior endeavors. You will also explore new sides of yourself, building financial and professional autonomy along the way. Someday, you might even wake up to find that as a result of all these adventures, you're a different person.

Thanks to his 10%, Dr. Patrick Linnenbank is now a lot like James Bond.

Except that he's a bit more interesting. Patrick, who is Dutch and lives in the Netherlands, runs his own counterterrorism and investigations firm and sits on the boards of a few human rights organizations. He's also got certifications in all kinds of esoteric disciplines, ranging from ethical hacking and Krav-Haganah to evasive driving and criminal profiling. His resumé makes him seem like a secret agent, but unless you're one of the bad guys, he's down-to-earth and very personable, as his two children will attest.

After medical school, Patrick realized that the life of a surgeon had one major drawback: you have to stay in one place—so he packed up, went to France, and completed an MBA. Since he would "go absolutely nuts" working only one job, after a year buried in PowerPoint presentations as a management consultant at Bain & Company, he picked up twenty-four hour shifts as an emergency room physician. Over the next decade, Patrick worked his way up to partner while saving lives on the side. That would be more than enough excitement for most people, but he also developed an interest in forensic medicine. It drew upon his medical training and allowed him to make a tangible contribution in the human rights arena, another passion. In the course of conducting mass-grave investigations in Africa, his life came under threat multiple times, so he next resolved to acquire expertise in security issues, gaining proficiency in sharpshooting, escaping from captivity, and all the other things you need to know to stay safe in some of the most dangerous corners of the globe.

Thanks to the skills he developed at his day job and on the side, Patrick is now the Founder of Seraph Protection Group, a firm that specializes in high-risk security, counterterrorism consulting, and forensic investigations. From its offices in Europe, Asia, Latin America, and China, the firm provides services to shipping corporations, NGOs, and high-net-worth individuals.

Still not content with just one job, he takes on consulting clients as well.

Patrick's story blew my mind. He wasn't just James Bond, he was also Jack Bauer, with a little *ER* and *CSI* thrown in. When you look at his LinkedIn profile, it's natural to feel somewhat intimidated. He's the type of guy who makes nearly everyone I know (myself included) look like a lazy sloth. Yet while he's clearly smart and driven, his success comes down to a simple fact: he's a master at getting the most out of time and money and he works hard to invest his resources wisely.

Patrick combined three seemingly disparate careers— medicine, forensics, and security—into one integrated portfolio. If you're wondering how he did it, as I did, the answer is straight-forward: like everybody else you'll meet in this book, he sat down, put pen to paper, and figured out how much of his time and financial capital he could free up and invest in entrepreneurial activities. Once he knew what he was working with, he pursued two key strategies. First, he focused on areas that were directly related to subjects in which he could already claim some intellectual capital. Jumping from medicine to forensics was a natural move and he was far more productive than if he had tried to become a cliff diver or a concert pianist. Next, where he didn't already have expertise, he methodically studied to attain the specific capabilities that would allow him to achieve his overall goals. Patrick recognized that he would need adequate training if he wanted to advance in the world of mass-grave forensics, so he invested his time and money very strategically to get the best instruction he could afford. In his case, that meant studying with antiterrorism experts in the United States, Israel, and Africa.

In this chapter, you will take stock of how you spend your time and your money. In doing so, you'll endeavor to make at least 10% of your time and financial capital available for the part of your career that exists outside of your day job. While that sounds like a big commitment if you're starting from scratch, you'll be surprised that, with some planning and prioritization, you can get more out of each of these resources. Remember, you're going to be working on projects that you enjoy and that will provide real benefits to your career and your life, so while you'll make some sacrifices, you'll get back much more than you give.

Time

Every 10% Entrepreneur I know talks about time, has a strategy for time, and wishes for more time. Whether they are single, married, stay-at-home parents, or working parents, they concentrate on balancing their personal and professional obligations. The good news and bad news is that twenty-four hours in a day is a global standard—there's nothing you can do to change that. So no matter if you're Steve Jobs or Steve the Slacker, you have the same number of hours to divide among all of your priorities.

Bear in mind, 10% is a target, but more than anything else, it's a mind-set. So while I'm not suggesting you should set aside one tenth of each working day for your side projects, you will need to make adjustments in order to free up time. You'll do that in several ways. First, you'll seek to achieve multiple objectives during one fixed period. Second, you'll eliminate activities that do not fit in with your priorities. Third, much like Patrick Linnenbank, you will pursue activities that build on your existing skills and advance your overarching objectives.

1. Make Time Count for More

The smarter your use of time, the better, so thinking about how to get more out of time is a 10% Entrepreneur's best friend. You might be tempted to multitask, cramming more into your day or shortchanging one activity for another. Don't text while you drive! I'm not a fan of multitasking—I need to focus to do things correctly and enjoy my work. I do believe, however, that you can use one period of time to achieve multiple objectives.

The secret is to combine passive activities—say folding laundry or exercising on the elliptical machine—with activities that require deeper thinking. If you've got work to do, you can make calls during your commute or during your lunch hour or coffee break. Why waste valuable time listening to the radio, playing games on your phone, or talking about the same old office politics when you can spend it doing something for yourself? You can also organize your thoughts while you're on your morning run or in the shower, and network for new opportunities with the other parents at your child's school play. All those activities contribute to your 10%, but you can seamlessly work them into the rest of your life. I know one guy who listens to podcasts about oil and gas when he walks the dog. He manages to keep up on energy-industry trends while taking Fido around the block.

It's worth remembering that many of us spend a good deal of our work hours waiting around for things to happen or sitting in endless meetings. Despite the remarkable gains in efficiency in the workplace in the past twenty years, most people still put in a minimum of forty hours a week at their job. That means that you can likely get far more out of the hours that you're at the office. During my first years on Wall Street, I became intimately acquainted with the concept of "face time." Face time is the unspoken expectation that an employee should be at his desk until the boss leaves, regardless of whether there's any actual work to do. It is an unfortunate practice that is elevated to an art form in most corporations. I once had a colleague who was always working late, often sending e-mails well past midnight. Our bosses were consistently impressed by his willingness to toil around the clock while the rest of us loafers were fast asleep. I was in awe of his seemingly prodigious work ethic until the day, years later, when I learned that he made a habit of prescheduling e-mails to go out at random hours of the night. It turns out that he was a master of "virtual" face time.

You can bet that Patrick Linnenbank doesn't do much face time. When he worked in consulting, he always overdelivered so that his colleagues wouldn't question his commitment, but he had too much going on to waste his time keeping up appearances. Depending on your job, your employer may very well be paying you for your output rather than by your actual hours. You don't get overtime when you respond to e-mails late at night or on the weekend, so why can't you find ways to set aside time for your 10% during the day? That's how many of the very busy people profiled in this book make their 10% work even when they've got demanding careers. Thanks to the veritable office you are carrying around in your smartphone, you can carve out a few minutes to type some e-mails, make a few calls, and take care of day-to-day activities during business hours.

It's important to emphasize that as you spend time on your 10%, there's one line that you should never cross: you must always prioritize your day job, especially during business hours. After all, it is the part of your life that will permit you to work on your own ventures in the first place. It gives you the stability and the cash flow to invest in yourself. If you fail to perform, you're putting your 10%, as well as the other 90%, on the line. It's not worth the risk and it's just not the way you want to operate. Respect your employer and the tools your company provides to you, including corporate e-mail. Treat them as sacrosanct and resist the temptation to use them for your own endeavors. Moreover, don't undertake any activities that violate the rules set down by your employer and never breach the conditions of your employment contract.

2. Cut Out the Noise and Focus

Think back, if you can, to the days before Facebook, Twitter, YouTube, Netflix, blogs, e-commerce sites, online newspapers, texting, and even e-mail. It's hard to remember what we did with all that free time. The average American spends roughly twenty-three hours a week e-mailing, texting, and using social media and other forms of online communication.[1] Citizens of the United Kingdom, Indonesia, the Philippines, China, Brazil, the United States, Nigeria, Colombia, Thailand, Saudi Arabia, South Africa, the Czech Republic, and Russia spend at least six hours a day looking at some sort of screen, whether it's television, a computer, a phone, or a tablet![2]

Cutting down on distractions and reallocating that mindshare to your 10% can be a transformative commitment. If you're like me, you waste precious minutes checking your e-mail, surfing the Web, and texting, all the while sacrificing productivity. Eliminating that noise will help you to focus, get organized, and find time to work. You don't have to lock yourself up in an isolated room to concentrate, but you do need to dedicate quality time to your efforts. That means cutting down on television, turning off your

The 10% Plan: Exercise 1—Managing Time

In order to better understand how you can make room for your 10%, keep a log of how you spend your time both in and out of the office. Do so for at least a week. The idea is to identify time in your day that you can repurpose for your 10% or that you can use for multiple objectives. Time with family, taking care of others, or taking care of yourself are nonnegotiable responsibilities, so they aren't mentioned here. Based on this rationale, monitor how much time you dedicate to the following types of activities:

- Commuting
- On the phone or texting
- Responding to personal e-mails
- On social media, reading news sites, or shopping online
- Watching television or movies
- Exercising
- Socializing with friends
- Eating out
- Other

Once you've taken stock of how you spend your time, look for ways to repurpose it. How much leisure time or free time are you willing to invest? Are there times in the day when you find yourself wasting time? Do you have space in your day to dedicate to your 10% without affecting your performance or causing friction with your employer?

phone, disabling notifications on your computer, and if possible, leaving the office during lunch to find a quiet place to work.

Prioritization also includes your health. People always tell you that you should never take your health for granted, but if you have not had more than a bad case of the flu, you can't imagine how it feels when your body suddenly turns against you. When you get sick, really sick, you finally get it. Until you are back on your feet, it's difficult to focus on much of anything else, let alone your career. You learn that if you're going to have the physical and mental strength to overcome challenges, pursue new ventures, and embrace change, you need to be strong. You're going to be far more productive if you take care of yourself, so eating well, sleeping on a normal schedule, and making time for exercise will help you feel your best and think more clearly. If you're looking for focus, you might also want to consider practicing meditation. A few minutes a day of focused quiet time can make a noticeable difference when it comes to your mental acuity.

3. Spend Your Time on Projects That Complement the Rest of Your Life

Whether you cut down on time online, watch less TV, or prioritize your 10% over other activities or hobbies, you will be far more likely to work efficiently and have fun if you choose ventures that play to your strengths and your interests. Patrick Linnenbank is a great example of how choosing the right areas of focus pays off. He leveraged the areas where he had strong intellectual capital to explore related specialties that excited him, and vice versa. His medical skills allowed him to study forensics. His interest in human rights compelled him to invest in security training. The intersection of those fields of knowledge provided him with the inspiration and the business plan for his own company, so in effect he went from strength to strength, adding intellectual capital while in pursuit of a larger goal.

Complementarity can also extend to the people you recruit to work alongside you. By partnering with those you like and respect, you can spend time with the important people in your life. If you opt for projects that involve your spouse or your children, your 10% will help you to maximize time with family. The same goes for friends or professional contacts. The teams at Bunny Inc., Monday Night Brewing, and Oyster Bay Brewing all started their companies based on personal relationships. The Founders wanted to find ways to collaborate, so when they came across an idea worth exploring, they did so as partners.

No matter how carefully you plan, at some point you may start to feel very busy. Remember, this is your 10%, designed by you, for you. You can customize it to fit the confines of your life, so you always have a choice. All the people in this book deal with trade-offs, conflicts, and horrible days when they feel like packing it in. They live 24/7 lives that are filled with family, travel, pets, hobbies, and all the other things that make our lives interesting and busy. But they are only human and they must all manage twenty-four hours in a day. If you feel like life is getting out of control, don't despair. You have the power to change things.

Financial Capital

Unlike time, which is sometimes hard to measure, money is pretty straightforward. When I first settled on a commitment of 10%, I did so partly because that level of engagement felt comfortable to me. As with an investment of my time, I felt that one tenth represented a meaningful, yet prudent, dedication of capital. It was only later that I discovered that my "gut" allocation was actually right in line with the market. According to the Kauffman Foundation, the average Angel allocates about 10% of his wealth to entrepreneurial ventures.[3]

Throughout this book, you'll see case studies and strategies that are relevant even if you have little or no money to set aside for your 10%. Still, some opportunities will only be available to you if you can bring cash to the table. As a result, your ultimate goal is to dedicate some part of your financial resources, ideally at least 10% of your wealth, to your work. In doing so, you can think of this commitment as a kind of tithe. With this tithe, however, the beneficiary will be your overall financial diversification and your future. Remember, you are formulating a long-term plan, so even if you cannot invest today, you can make preparations that will allow you to do so down the line.

Apart from generating financial returns, investing allows you to diversify yourself, not just with respect to your career, but also in relation to the other holdings in your portfolio. For many people, the most significant investment is their home. A recent New York University study revealed that the richest 1 percent of Americans have 9 percent of their wealth invested in their homes. For the broader middle class, however, approximately 63 percent of household net worth is tied up in housing. As you know, having a concentrated position in one investment is risky, especially when you consider that the last financial crisis hit homeowners hardest. Before you decide to add another room onto your house, it's worth considering how you can diversify your finances by earmarking that cash for your 10% instead.[4]

So how do you actually go about setting aside financial capital? On a day-to-day basis, managing money, much like managing time, is about making choices. By taking a look at how you spend your money and invest your savings, you can devise a plan to free up financial capital so that you can invest in side projects either today or in the future.

It's amazing how quickly expenses, even the little things, add up. The average American spends more than $1,000 per year on coffee, roughly 1 percent of earnings on alcohol,[5] and more than 5 percent of wages on eating out.[6] The cost of a cable television bundle now exceeds $1,200 per year. When I got a bill for $200 for a month of cable, thanks to going a little crazy with premium

The 10% Plan: Exercise 2—Managing Financial Capital

Prepare a personal financial statement, preferably on a spreadsheet, detailing your financial capital. Project those balances forward for a period of five years, adding any expected significant changes in your finances, such as increased financial resources due to a promotion, a bonus, or the proceeds from the sale of an asset such as a house or car. Adjust these projections for any expected investments, such as buying a house, paying for schooling for yourself or others, or making any significant purchases. Based on this five-year projection, calculate the following:

- How much capital can you set aside now for your 10%?
- How much capital will you have in five years for your 10%?

Next, prepare a personal budget. After you pay expenses, how much do you have left over, if anything, to increase your savings? What changes can you make to free up money for your 10% on an annual basis?

Please see the appendix for templates that will guide you as you calculate your base of financial capital and prepare a personal budget.

channels that I barely watched, I decided to cut the cord. I now direct the savings to my 10%. I have much more fun building my 10% than flipping through dozens of channels looking for something decent to watch.

Saving doesn't mean you have to radically change your daily routine and suck all the fun out of life. It does mean that you need to free up some cash, either by drawing upon your existing savings and investments or by cutting costs and saving more.[7] Over time, you will put your financial capital to work to create a portfolio of discrete investments, often reinvesting any proceeds you generate. In order to begin that process of saving and investing, you will need to understand your current financial picture as well as your capacity to save.

You've Got Money to Invest—Now What?

No matter whether you're putting 1 percent or 100 percent of your financial capital into a given opportunity, not every investment offers the same degree of risk and return. Investing your money in real estate is a very different undertaking than financing the entrepreneur who plans to market Tinder for dogs. One of those investments is relatively safe, highly predictable, and pretty easy to value. The other is . . . Tinder for dogs. Depending on your level of risk tolerance, you may never sleep again if you commit your money to investments that you perceive to be speculative. You've got to be comfortable with the risks that you're taking with each and every investment.

One of your principal objectives for your 10% is to create upside. If you're investing financial capital as an Angel, you make cash investments in promising businesses with the expectation of generating future profits. So what should you expect in terms of return on investment? In an extensive fifteen-year study of returns to angel investors based on a database of some 1,200 investments, the Kauffman Foundation found that on a portfolio level, investors made 2.5 times their money over a 3.5-year period. That represents a return of approximately 30 percent per annum. Meanwhile, a survey of twelve studies compiled by venture capitalist David Teten illustrates that angels can expect returns of anywhere from 18 percent to 54 percent on an annualized basis.[8]

Those results are compelling, especially when you consider that stocks generate expected long-term returns of around 10 percent a year, while holding cash produces an annual return of 3.5 percent.[9] Even if you assume a steep discount to all these studies, the point remains the same. Over a ten-year period, the numbers add up: a diversified portfolio of angel investments can generate more than ten times what you'd get from holding cash and more than five times what you'd get in the stock market. That said, all these studies track returns at a portfolio level. That means that some of the investments in a portfolio will perform much better than the average while others will be complete failures. For that reason, prudent investors seek to create portfolios, rather than just investing in one or two companies, over the course of their careers.

Whether you have $5,000 or $100,000 to invest per year, you are going to construct your portfolio with several guiding principals in mind. First, while your 10% is the place for you to generate upside, you won't do so at the expense of your overall financial health. Never invest money that you cannot afford to commit to long-term ventures that entail some risk. That's the beauty of sticking to 10%—you don't throw all of your eggs into one basket. Second, strive for diversification over the long run. Endeavor to add different types of assets and projects to your 10% in order to create a portfolio of investments. For example, if you're an Angel, you can vary the types of investments you make with respect to the industry or the maturity of the business. Also, by growing the number of investments in your portfolio over time, you will increase diversification, lower risk, and enhance your chances of picking winners.

You can also supplement your capital with Advisor roles. Whether you are investing financial capital or intellectual capital, you're still making an investment. The difference, of course, is that when you invest intellectual capital, the risks are limited to your time and not your wallet. If you are investing cash in addition to your time, you will find that being an Angel and an Advisor in the same company has clear benefits. As an Advisor you work alongside management to make their company more successful. That benefits all of your shares, whether you got them as an Angel or an Advisor, so you will maximize your combined return.

Your 10% is a tool for diversification, but it's also an opportunity to talk about risk with the other people who are stakeholders in your life. You want to have autonomy, but not at the expense of your relationships. That's why it's important to talk through your investment strategy with anyone, such as a significant other, who shares his or her financial destiny with you. Together, you can reach a common agreement about how much risk you are willing to accept. Based on that understanding, you can vary the type of investments you're making in order to balance the risk in your portfolio.

Now that you've taken stock of the time and financial capital that you can invest in your 10%, it's time to turn your attention to intellectual capital. Although setting out to measure your skills and expertise in a given area may seem like a more nebulous concept than counting hours or money, intellectual capital is an equally important resource. As you will see in the next chapter, if you invest your intellectual capital wisely, you will get more out of your time and financial capital. You will also generate incremental returns on your investment, returns that are not measured in monetary terms but rather in the form of experiences and the thrill of doing something you enjoy. The key to creating an ongoing supply of both financial and nonfinancial returns is to choose projects that play to your strengths and your passions.

Chapter 6

Playing to Your Strengths

The poem "The Summer Day" by Mary Oliver concludes:[1]

Tell me, what is it you plan to do
With your one wild and precious life?

If you were to answer that question every New Year's Day, the collected responses, over decades, would tell the story of your life. Youthful exuberance would yield to practical considerations. Along the way, your priorities would shift, a by-product of wisdom and the lessons life teaches, whether you want to learn them or not. That's only natural, and mostly unavoidable. At the same time, you can lose touch with some of the things that were once critical to you without even noticing. You cede ground slowly, almost imperceptibly. Most of us don't take the time to reflect as much as we should, and when we look back, we see that we've drifted away from once important ideas or pursuits as a result of circumstance rather than choice.

Your 10% is not about eating your broccoli. It isn't about what you *should* do, but rather what you *want* to do. Integrating entrepreneurship into your life while keeping your day job means that you can afford to take some risks and think of life as wild and precious if you'd like. You can also find something you love, try something you've always dreamed of pursuing, or explore something new. Even if things don't work out, you've got a pretty great backup plan—your day job. No matter what happens, you'll learn, develop valuable skills, meet new people, and answer that nagging question: what if? You'll also still have a roof over your head and everything else you value to fall back on. As you follow your passions, you'll want to make the most of an all-important resource: intellectual capital, as it's the factor that will most directly shape your answer to Mary Oliver's question.

In this chapter, you're going to focus on generating two sets of ideas. First, you'll explore your interests in order to develop a clearer sense of where to concentrate your efforts as you build your 10%. Even if you suspect that you already know the answer, give yourself the space to cast a wide net. Ideas or opportunities that once seemed impractical as full-time pursuits may now make sense, so this is the time to keep an open mind and explore all of your options. You'll have plenty of time to narrow your focus later.

Once you generate a list of areas to explore, you'll turn to intellectual capital. Your skills and experience will allow you to make smart decisions, to go from strength to strength, and to engage meaningfully and contribute to the success of each of your ventures. Whether you draw from your day job, your education, or your hobbies, everything you've learned until now is fair game, as they are all part of your base of intellectual capital.

Let's get started by stepping back and cleaning the slate. You may have some ideas for your 10%, or you may not, but either way there's no need to set anything in stone at the moment. As you read this, you have no limits and nothing to lose. The only resources you are committing are your time and your intellect, so you can think freely about what you actually want to do.

Economists think in terms of "opportunity cost" in order to measure what you give up by choosing one alternative over another. It's calculated by adding up the value of the benefits that you forgo as a result of making a choice. For example, if you quit your job to start a company, your opportunity cost would be the compensation you left behind. This approach allows you to quantify the impact of your decisions, at least in terms of your finances. It also helps to explain why so many people find it hard to make changes in their careers. When opportunity cost is high, you can wake up one day and find yourself locked in golden handcuffs.

Opportunity cost is kind of like gravity. It keeps your head out of the clouds and your feet planted firmly on the ground. But since the purpose of this exercise is to do exactly the opposite, let's suspend reality for a little while. What happens when you flip the notion of opportunity cost on its head? Imagine you show up to work tomorrow and find a padlock on the front door of the building. Since your opportunity cost—the cost of simply walking away from your current job—is now zero, you can plot a path forward with nothing from your old firm to encumber you. If you had to press the reset button, what would you want to do?

The first step is to make a list of the kinds of professional opportunities you'd like to pursue next. As you generate ideas that interest and excite you, feel free to dream, to think outside of your day job, and to explore all those ideas that you've kept tucked away for a rainy day. I'm going to throw down just one basic rule to keep in mind as you work on the Opportunity Cost Zero exercise on the following page. Connect your thinking to the intellectual capital that you have today or could reasonably acquire in the foreseeable future. It's great to let your feet leave the ground, but you don't want to go way up into the stratosphere without an oxygen tank. So unless you've got catlike quickness, or you can cry on command, cross off Olympic sprinter and actor from your list. Beyond that, don't worry about any other factors, say financial or logistical constraints, that could impede you. There's plenty of time to dwell on limitations, so try to disregard them for the moment. You cannot draw boundaries on a map before you've drawn the map itself, so permit yourself to think in terms of potential rather than strict practicality. As long as you've got the skills to make a run at something, consider it fair game.

The list of ideas from the exercise will stand independent of your day-to-day responsibilities, your job title, or the nagging doubts that can cause you to question whether you should just go for it. The idea is for each item on the list to feel completely natural, almost organic, within the context of your interests and skills. It's a list of ideas that will resonate with you and with people who know you well. If you were to show your parent, significant other, mentor, or best friend what you've included on your list, he or she would smile and say, "Of course . . . that makes complete sense."

The 10% Plan: Exercise 3—Opportunity Cost Zero: What Do You Want to Do?

Thinking in terms of opportunity cost permits you to step outside of the responsibilities and tasks of your day job and instead focus on what you enjoy, your talents, and your dreams to answer the question "What do you want to do?" One of the best ways to structure your thinking is by answering a series of questions that can help you uncover your interests. As you work through this exercise, take notes, as you will be returning to these answers later on.

To get started, answer the following questions:

- How do you like to spend your time at work?
- What day-to-day tasks do you enjoy?
- What talents do you have that are special and that set you apart?
- Do you prefer working on a team or working alone?
- What kinds of problems do you like to solve?
- Do you prefer to advise or to lead?
- Do you like doing one thing or do you prefer variety?
- What do you do best at your job? Where do you struggle?
- What do you like about your job? What do you dislike?
- What have been your most enjoyable professional experiences?
- If you had to do one thing for the rest of your life, what would it be?
- What were your favorite classes in school?
- What did you want to do for a living when you were sixteen? When you were twenty-five?
- Whom do you admire professionally?
- Whose job do you wish you had?
- Are there any business ideas that you just can't get out of your head?

- What would your mentors or friends say are your ideal jobs or roles?
- What do you like to read? What subjects or fields do you follow in the news?

Now, based on your responses to the questions above, answer the following questions, in order to generate a list of industries, roles, or professional areas that appeal to you:

- What kinds of business opportunities would you like to pursue? What industries or business models excite you?
- Who are the people with whom you would like to work?
- What kinds of skills do you want to acquire?
- What skills can you bring to a business venture?
- What's your dream project?
- Do you prefer to lead, advise, or be an equal partner?

Fitting New Opportunities into a Crowded Life

When I was in my second year of business school I took an advanced competitive strategy class. The somewhat cryptic subtitle of the class was "Integrating the Enterprise."[2] Over the course of the semester, I discovered that those three words—"integrating the enterprise"—hinted at a powerful insight: in order for a business to be successful, all of its activities must come together in a cohesive fashion. Through careful attention to strategy, smart companies structure themselves around a self-reinforcing and virtuous cycle of activities. Each part of the business is better because of its overarching design. It may seem like a simple concept, but I'd never before thought of businesses as integrated machines.

Companies with tightly integrated strategies are like elite runners. When you observe world-class marathoners, their movements look, in a sense, somewhat mechanical. Each movement contributes to propelling the athlete's body closer to the finish line. If the subcomponents of the runner's form—the strike of the foot or the swing of the arms—complement each other, then less effort is needed to fly forward. With efficiency comes speed, but since all the elements of the form are moving in alignment, the risk of injury also declines. This is a virtuous cycle, after all. Thanks to an economy of motion and a unity of purpose, the runner integrates the entire undertaking.

Thinking about how an elite runner moves her body, or how the components of a machine come together to complete a task, apply this same precision to your 10%. Each decision, endeavor, and action should contribute to the overall strategy. The more tightly you can align your intellectual capital, together with your professional interests, passions, and relationships, into your 10%, the more you can achieve with each and every action. Greater alignment with the other 90% also increases the chance that you will find success and fulfillment in all 100%. It adds fuel to the machine.

How will you know that you're on the path to aligning all these factors? You'll feel it intuitively as you start working on projects that offer you the autonomy that comes with entrepreneurship. The time and effort won't feel like "work," even though, of course, you will be doing all kinds of work. You will analyze business opportunities, conduct research, formulate decisions, make connections, and set aside time for conference calls and meetings. Drawing on your intellectual capital, you will ask lots of questions of yourself and others, all the while pushing yourself outside of your comfort zone. You will deal with uncertainty and risk, struggle with gray areas, and sometimes you'll have to trust your gut. You will have successes and you will have failures, and there will be surprises, both good and bad. That's just part of the process of building businesses. That's how you plant seeds. Yet none of this will feel like work because every one of these activities will come as a result of a series of choices you have made.

Dipali Patwa's 10% served as a catalyst for her to pursue her passions while integrating them into a busy life. Her children's clothing line feels as if it could only have come from someone who arrived in Brooklyn by way of Mumbai. The children jamming the pages of the Masala Baby catalog express the diversity of Dipali's adopted city, yet a common strand unites them: they are dressed in the colors and designs of her native India. Her catalog models include her son, Elan, and all the Masala kids she bumps into around the halls of her apartment building.

As a young design-school graduate, Dipali traveled throughout rural India, living in villages for months at a time and nurturing a deep appreciation for her country's design heritage. Thanks to a fellowship, she found her way to New York, and when she decided to stay, she embarked on a lifelong mission to fuse the unique qualities of India with those of her new home. That wasn't going to happen overnight, so she spent a decade working in the home fashion decor industry, slowly building intellectual capital and credibility.

After starting a family, Dipali stumbled upon a promising opportunity to reconnect with India in the nursery of her very own apartment. Whenever she dressed her son in clothing her mom sent from India, the outfits got rave reviews. Maybe there was a way to inject Indian design sensibility into the booming market for specialty children's products? On an investment of $5,000, Dipali developed a line of ten baby items and secured a booth at a children's clothing tradeshow to test and validate her idea. From day one, it was a hit. Before long, she was running sales out of her bedroom, storing inventory in the basement, and spending her free time shipping a growing line of products to boutiques all over the United States.

By its fifth year of operations, Masala Baby designed and sourced more than a thousand items per season. Now that her clients and Elan are growing up, Dipali has expanded the line into kid's fashions as well. The company sells online, through more than 250 specialty stores, and at large retailers like Nordstrom. The entire product line is made in India and sourced from fair trade and organic suppliers whenever possible. Dipali also seeks to foster female entrepreneurship, and many of her manufacturing partners are women. As the brand's visibility grows, Dipali finds Masala Baby popping up in surprising places. When fashion bloggers spotted Matthew McConaughey's son, Levi, wearing a Masala Baby tunic in *People* magazine, she sold out of that item overnight.

Given Masala Baby's success and the growing demands of her 10%, Dipali eventually decided to rebalance her career. She left her full-time job to split her time evenly between Masala Baby and a role as chief creative officer of Mela Artisans, a company that imports ethically sourced artisanal products from India to the United States. Masala Baby and Mela share a common vision and overlapping values, so she finds managing both sets of responsibilities to be intense but achievable, given the clear synergies at hand. She's also purposefully minimized the friction between her two sets of responsibilities. Masala Baby's team sits just down the hall from Mela.

Thanks to some thoughtful planning, Dipali has shown herself to be a designer whose talent for fusion goes far beyond fabrics. Her passions for family, fashion, India, and entrepreneurship now coalesce to reflect her particular skills and ambitions. As Dipali can attest, when your intellectual capital and passions intersect, you can feel it. You become hyperefficient, fully aligned, and highly productive because you know that you're doing what you're meant to be doing. She works hard, but Masala Baby is a reflection of everything that matters to her, so integrating the company with the rest of her life just makes sense.

Although Dipali's journey from designer to entrepreneur seems entirely organic in retrospect, she, like any first-time entrepreneur, worked hard to find an idea that excited her while still building on her professional strengths. She thought carefully about her skills as well as her passions, so that when the Masala Baby concept popped into her head, she was both excited and well prepared to invest a little time and money to test her idea.

If you don't have any business ideas in mind, or you have greater conviction about your passions than your skills, or vice versa, don't be discouraged. Brilliant ideas rarely fall out of the sky, so figuring out how to tap into your experiences and interests requires some homework. Just remember that entrepreneurs come from a wide range of industries and backgrounds, so you don't need any specific type of experience. Rather, the key is to identify the areas where you are most proficient and then seek out opportunities that leverage your abilities.

To Know Where You're Going, Look at Where You've Been

When you've been working in the same industry or role for a while, you can forget that many of the things you do on a daily basis are actually pretty unique. If you're sitting in an office building with a thousand other people who are really good at making spreadsheets in Excel, you might forget that, in the outside world, lots of people find spreadsheets completely terrifying. It's funny how skills that you once worked hard to learn can come to feel like they are mundane. When you break away from your tribe and leave the confines of your routine, you'll discover that your intellectual capital won't be taken for granted. The lawyer is amazed by the accountant's ability to create spreadsheets out of thin air. The accountant cannot get over the designer's ability to conjure up ideas and blend form with function. This same phenomenon extends to a wide range of disciplines, like IT, marketing, the arts, carpentry, and any other field that requires specialized skills.

In the Opportunity Cost Zero exercise, you spent some time away from the boundaries of your daily life to explore the question "What do you want to do?" Now it's time to begin narrowing down the long list of ideas in order to focus on those areas that play to your strengths. To do so, you will answer another question: "What do you do well?" This is where intellectual capital comes into the picture.

Even though most people have put together a resumé at one time or another, pinpointing and synthesizing what you're good at, specifically your intellectual capital, can be more difficult than you'd think. When I was getting started as a 10% Entrepreneur, I struggled to articulate my intentions and my skills to friends, family, and most important, the community of people who could help me make some progress. I wasn't helping my case. I was disorganized, I hadn't taken time to set objectives, and while I generally knew of some areas that interested me professionally, I hadn't really considered all the possibilities. The good news is that if you've done the exercises in the first half of this book, you've already tackled those challenges, so you are a number of steps ahead of where I found myself.

Since I wasn't quite there yet, when it came to communicating my professional strengths, I didn't know how to put all I'd done in my career into context. I could talk about some accomplishments, but my ad hoc list of credentials was far from comprehensive or connected. I tended to remember the past few years of work experiences, but I didn't think back to earlier times, to formative roles and relationships, to see how everything came together.

My lack of focus was a severe limitation. That became abundantly clear when I approached my friend Kenna, who is an executive recruiter, for advice. When we met, she asked me to summarize my background and my strengths, so I opened my mouth and didn't stop talking for the next five minutes. I listed a bunch of seemingly unrelated interests, detailed some previous jobs, and threw in a random fact or two about projects I had worked on in places like Pakistan, Turkey, and Colombia. After I finally stopped talking, Kenna raised her eyebrows, blinked a few times, and offered me some advice: "Patrick, resist the temptation to tell me everything you've ever done. It's interesting, but it's a little overwhelming. Instead, know your audience and what is relevant to them and then tailor your message accordingly. Think of everything else you've done as a surprise that you can whip out someday in the future if and when it's pertinent to the conversation."

I blushed and thanked her. I was all over the map, both literally and figuratively, and if I was going to tell and sell my story, I needed to speak with authority, clarity, and most important, focus. Over lunch a few weeks later, a friend from college, Katherine, unexpectedly threw me a lifeline. She mentioned that she ran into another of our contemporaries from college, Mark Vlasic, who was practicing law in Washington, D.C., and was involved in all kinds of meaningful side projects. If I needed a little inspiration, she suggested, I should read the biography on his Web site.

She was right. In addition to his legal career, I discovered that Mark had served as a White House Fellow, prosecuted war crimes at the Hague, and appeared as an expert commentator on major television networks. As I read, two thoughts crossed my mind. First, I should get up earlier in the morning and do more with my days. Mark gives Patrick Linnenbank a run for his money when it comes to getting things done. Second, few people bother to put together a biography, much less a comprehensive one. Yet compared to a resumé, Mark's approach worked better because he achieved three objectives. First, he provided a comprehensive summary of all his experiences and framed them for the reader in support of his overarching goals. Second, he established instant credibility. Finally, he laid out his strengths and areas of expertise with precision, so that most anyone operating in his field could think of multiple ways they could work together.

1. Tell Your Story on Your Own Terms

If you rely solely on a resumé, you're missing an opportunity to own the narrative. A resumé is no more than a laundry list of jobs, skills, and educational accomplishments. There is no context, no perspective, and no story line that links all of your experiences so that they make sense to the reader. If you've moved around a lot, lost a job, or transitioned to a new industry, there's no way to convey the reasons or the benefits of your actions. Instead, the reader is left to his own devices. A biography, on the other hand, is the story of your life, told and framed by you. You control the message, so you can emphasize what you feel is most important.

2. Establish Credibility from the Start

When you're meeting new people, you need an effective way to build credibility early on. You want to be taken seriously and use everyone's time as efficiently as possible. Nevertheless, you wouldn't send someone a copy of your resumé unless you were looking for a job. That means that you need some other way to make it clear that you've got something real to offer, so that you stand out from the crowd and save precious time detailing your skills and experiences. By preparing a biography that you can either share via e-mail or post online, for example, on LinkedIn, you can explain your past and highlight your achievements without feeling uncomfortable or awkward about putting yourself out there. Your bio will do all the talking.

3. Identify Areas of Expertise and Intellectual Capital

Most important, preparing a biography benefits *you*. Even though it's important to tell the outside world where your strengths lie, you also need to get your story straight, especially for yourself. By stepping back, you can take stock of your past, and then figure out what that means for your future. As you trace the threads, themes, and areas where you possess intellectual capital, you will inform your thinking for when it comes time to draw on your intellectual capital and apply it to your 10%. You can also allow yourself to feel proud of what you've done. It's good to stop every once in a while and remember that you've been building something that uniquely reflects your efforts and talents. Appreciate

The 10% Plan: Exercise 4—Writing Your Professional Biography: Your Intellectual Capital

Make a list of the following, using your resumé as a guide (and if you haven't updated your resumé lately, tackle that task first):

- Academic credentials
- Employers and roles
- Core skills
- Accomplishments and awards
- Key clients and relationships
- Leadership and management experiences
- Courses, training, and certifications
- Community activities
- Hobbies
- Publications and research projects
- Professional organizations

Once you have a list of all of your professional achievements and experiences, organize them into four sections:

1. Professional experiences
2. Skills, credentials, and awards
3. Academic history
4. Personal interests and experiences

Draft a comprehensive biography that covers the four sections listed above. Refine and edit until you present a straightforward, cohesive history of your career and achievements that highlights your strengths. Give it to a few people you trust and ask them for their feedback. Which themes stand out? What do they perceive as your strengths? If they were starting a company and looking for talent, how would they fit you into their team?

> Based on this feedback, revise accordingly, until you successfully communicate the messages that you want to come across to the reader. When you have completed the comprehensive biography, prepare a shorter, more focused, version.
>
> Now, using your biography, make a list of the things that you do well, the specific skills you can offer to others, and the areas where you excel or stand out.
>
> Please see the appendix at the end of this book for a sample biography that you can use as a model.

all of your hard work—you've probably done a lot more than you remembered when you first sat down to write.

After I set aside time to take stock of my past, I ultimately prepared two biographies. The first was long, exhaustive, and would probably make my friends' eyes roll. I kept that one for myself, so that I could maintain a comprehensive list of all the skills and relationships I could bring to my 10%. Plus, whenever I felt lost, I could return to my biography for guidance. Next, I wrote a second, more focused one. This would be my calling card to share with anyone who could help me, and it would allow me to quickly establish credibility when looking for projects and partners. I also posted it to my LinkedIn profile. As someone who uses the site on a daily basis, I know it is inevitable that people will search for me there before agreeing to a meeting or a call.

Playing to Your Strengths

In this chapter, you completed two exercises. The first, Opportunity Cost Zero, sought to expand your horizons. The second,

Writing Your Professional Biography, was all about surfacing and contextualizing what you bring to the table. As a result of this work, you can now answer the following two questions:

1. What do you want to do?
2. What do you do well?

The intersection of the answers to these questions represents your sweet spot. In a general sense, it's the place where you will play to your strengths by pursuing projects that make the most effective use of your intellectual capital, while appealing to your interests. It's also a filter that you will apply as you consider how intellectual capital helps you to screen potential opportunities. Going forward, you will regard each endeavor through a focused lens to ask: Does it play to my strengths?

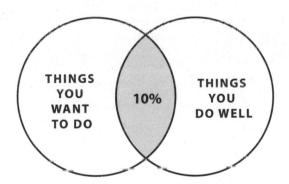

Take the case of Roberto Rittes. Roberto is not the kind of person who shies away from a challenge, even if it took awhile for him to figure out how to integrate entrepreneurship into his career. He's been to more than a hundred countries and was once the bodyboarding champion for the state of São Paulo, Brazil. Even though he's a thrill seeker, he never wanted to be a full-time entrepreneur. He preferred a more stable, predictable path, choosing corporate roles in finance and marketing, before landing at Oi, the largest telecom company in Brazil and South America. As general manager of Oi Paggo, a mobile payments business that was incubated within the company, he got to run a startup from the offices of an established industry leader. The experience was transformative, and he came away with an entirely new set of intellectual capital.

His eyes now open to the excitement of entrepreneurship, Roberto was a natural to become a 10% Entrepreneur, although it took him some time to find his footing. He explored a few ideas as a Founder, but he couldn't find an idea that got him truly excited. He also realized that it's hard to travel the world in search of adventure when you're running an early-stage company. Instead, Roberto opted to spread his bets as an Angel, investing in companies that play to his strengths and his passions. He's a huge fan of design, so he backed a retailer that is bringing affordable designer furniture to Brazil by partnering with local producers. As an Angel, he leverages his finance and strategy expertise, coupled with the lessons he picked up while launching the payments startup, to take an active role in mentoring the team. He also invested in a telecom business that draws directly on the intellectual capital he acquired both at Oi and at his current employer. He understands the business intuitively and can contribute directly to the company's dynamism and growth.

Returning to the work you've done in this chapter, study your responses to the Opportunity Cost Zero exercise and then reread your professional biography. As you do so, look for areas where you'll be playing to your strengths. The things you're good at will give you the key to opening the door to the things you enjoy. It's entirely possible to find yourself at the intersection of the things you want to do and the things you do well—that's how you craft a tightly integrated strategy. All the people you have met so far, as well as the people you are going to meet later in this book, found opportunities that play to their strengths. Dipali drew on her experience with textiles to explore her passion for Indian design. Roberto applied his considerable operational experience to the challenges of a startup whose focus on design excited him. For each of the individuals I've profiled, their 10% ties back to their interests, their personal stories, and their skills so much so that it's hard to imagine them *not* doing these things. When you meet someone like Luke of Luke's Lobster, you can't help but think that he was born to build his company. It's an extension of everything he is as a person.

Playing to your strengths can make an impact that goes well beyond yourself. You can also use your talents to work on projects that achieve broader objectives that are important to you. Given that women occupy just 15 percent of senior positions at venture capital firms, it isn't too surprising that female entrepreneurs often struggle to raise capital.[3] Anu Duggal saw too many great ideas fall through the cracks, so she created the Female Founders Fund, or F Cubed, specifically to back women entrepreneurs. For Anu, targeting women-led startups is just good business. She can generate higher returns by investing in companies that are overlooked by the rest of the industry. Although running F Cubed is a full-time endeavor, Anu's investor base includes a number of 10% Entrepreneurs and 110% Entrepreneurs who are executives and founders at firms like Gilt, Facebook, Google, and Netflix. They are eager to support female entrepreneurs while also making smart investment decisions. In fact, two of the 10% Entrepreneurs you met earlier are active members of the F Cubed network. Beth Ferreira sits on the

F Cubed investment committee, and Farah Khan has invested alongside Anu in one of her most promising portfolio companies.

Just because you're doing something good for the world doesn't mean that you cannot make money at the same time. For all the women (and men) in the F Cubed network, investing in promising female-led companies achieves multiple objectives, but it doesn't entail taking on incremental risk or generating a lower return than any comparable opportunity. Likewise, even as you build the best team possible, you can also use your 10% to invest back into your homeland, like Alex and Tania of Bunny Inc., or to create jobs in your home state, like Luke of Luke's Lobster. You can also choose to build a socially responsible venture, like Masala Baby, that integrates its social mission into its identity. All these 10% Entrepreneurs use business as a conduit to improve the world around them while pursuing strategies and objectives that contribute to their companies' overall financial success.

Of course, you may decide to pursue opportunities that don't yet fully play to your strengths. It's possible that you have a promising idea that falls outside of the intersection of your intellectual capital and your interests. After all, your 10% is a place to take some calculated risks, since you're doing so from a position of stability. By design, you'll be starting small so that you can learn by doing. You can then increase the size of your investment as you gain confidence and intellectual capital in a given area. When experimenting in your 10%, there are ways to avoid making the kinds of mistakes that are always more likely to occur when you are operating outside of your core areas of expertise. The simplest way is to partner with other people who have intellectual capital in areas where you do not. You will teach each other, you will learn, and you will increase the chance of success. In addition, you will be ready to take a more independent role the next time around.

If you're good at building financial projections and you want to work with restaurants, then you can look for projects that lie at the intersection of finance and cuisine, like helping a chef prepare a business plan for her new restaurant. When you're ready to get started, you can call someone like Dan Gertsacov at La Xarcuteria and find out if he needs help. Similarly, if you've got experience in social media marketing and you want to learn about startups in the travel space, then you can track down people like Diego Saez-Gil and Tomi Pierucci, who are working hard to execute their vision for Bluesmart and are looking for people to join the cause.

I got into the commercial real estate game thanks to my friend Jason who is a real estate investor in Miami. A few years ago, I got wind of the fact that a company I'd worked with in the past was seeking an investor for their Miami warehouse. I knew the company and the building well, and although I didn't know much about real estate, I knew whom to call. Jason lives less than twenty miles from the building, he was an experienced investor, and I trusted him like family. In this instance, our intellectual capital was highly complementary. I could vouch for the company and its owners while Jason could run the deal. Together, we put together what ended up being a terrific investment. Now that I've learned something about real estate, I've gone on to invest in two more of Jason's deals.

By virtue of working and partnering with people whose intellectual capital complements your own, you can count on them to extend your range. You can also return the favor, drawing on your particular skills to help others to expand their activities into new areas. That's the value of having a team. No matter how good you are at your job or how deep your experience, the right partner or partners can make a big difference. As you'll see later, nobody can know everything, and you'll draw upon your intellectual capital, as well as the smarts of the people in your network, to do your homework and find the answers. But before you mobilize your network, you need a process to find, analyze, and commit to opportunities. In the next chapter, you'll learn how to do the work of a 10% Entrepreneur, from finding your first projects and assessing their merits to structuring your involvement in each venture.

Chapter 7

Finding, Analyzing, and Committing to Ventures

N ow that you've taken stock of your resources, it's time to move on to the next stage of your 10% Plan. The investment process is the aspect of the plan that will guide you through each step as you identify and evaluate the ventures that will become part of your 10%. When you have questions, face doubts, or need to check your compass to make sure that you're still on course, it will help you to ask the right questions, search for answers, and then make decisions based on facts and data. Once you get the hang of it, the process is entirely replicable and will save you a lot of mental energy. By following the same series of steps, you will come to trust in your judgment, learn to work efficiently, and engage in projects that make the best use of your resources. You will also spend a lot of time out in the real world, getting your hands dirty and, in the process, thinking like a venture capitalist. That's the fun part of your work and it's often the most unpredictable. You never quite know where your 10%

will take you and you might very well find yourself in some un-expected places.

That's how I ended up at Playlist Live, a mammoth YouTube celebrity convention held in Orlando, Florida. If you've never been to one, let me tell you what you're missing. Walking around the event feels like you're surfing the Web, but in real life. You-Tube personalities sign autographs, sell T-shirts, and mix with their fans. The fans, a combination of tweens and techies, are in ecstasy since they are no longer limited to clicking "like" to show their adulation. It's hard not to get caught up in the spirit, so I was a bit starstruck when I met Tay Zonday, one of the first breakout YouTube stars. His "Chocolate Rain" video has gener-ated more than 100 million views, at least twenty of which can be traced to my IP address.

I flew to Orlando at the invitation of a former colleague, Mar-celo Camberos, who'd recently launched a company, Real Influ-ence, to partner consumer brands with YouTube celebrities. This was 2011, back in the Dark Ages of YouTube stardom. The idea was still in its infancy, and Marcelo was a pioneer. He needed a hand with business development, so he offered me an Advisor role in exchange for some equity and a commission on any sales I generated. Since I'd never worked on an entrepreneurial ven-ture from inception, I knew that at a minimum I would learn something new, in addition to having fun and reconnecting with a friend.

By offering me my first side project, Marcelo officially put me in business as a 10% Entrepreneur. He also put me through my paces. Having worked at online-entertainment pioneer Funny or Die, he was an expert when it came to video, and he taught me how to pitch this new marketing channel to potential clients. I'd never sold anything in my life, yet all of a sudden I was sitting across the table from serious companies like Diageo and Estée Lauder. It was humbling to be turned down and infuriating to be ignored, but we managed to close some sales. Still, the idea was ahead of its time and Marcelo eventually decided to shift his efforts to a venture he was forming with a rising YouTube superstar. I sold my Advisor shares back to the company, a little richer for my efforts and far more confident that I could think like an entrepreneur. Although I didn't realize it at the time, I'd also planted a seed for a future 10% venture.

When Marcelo called six months later to ask me if I wanted to invest in his new company, ipsy, I was intrigued. He was partnering with Michelle Phan, the biggest YouTube star in the beauty space, to create a subscription cosmetics business. I quickly realized I was well positioned to judge whether the business could work. Thanks to my time at Real Influence, I grasped the tremendous commercial potential that resides within YouTube, especially for its biggest celebrities, and I knew that Marcelo had the goods to execute. In a sense, I was just like the 71 percent of entrepreneurs surveyed by *Inc.* magazine who found their entrepreneurial idea while working at a previous job.

That wasn't the only factor at play. I discovered that I already knew another of ipsy's investors. When I was an Advisor at Real Influence, I introduced Marcelo to a former classmate, Nir Liberboim, so that we could learn from his experience working in the cosmetics industry. Since ipsy was all about the beauty sector, Marcelo had asked Nir to consider backing him. I trusted Nir's judgment, especially with regard to consumer businesses, so his decision to invest signaled a strong endorsement.

Even though I was excited, I still analyzed the opportunity as I would have any other investment I've made over the course of my career. I kept a cool head and did my homework in order to develop confidence in the team, the product, the investors, and my own ability to help make ipsy a success. Once I had conviction that I'd asked all the right questions, I signed the papers, wired the money, and the rest is history. In the next three years, on an investment of just a few million dollars, the company grew nearly 3,000 percent to more than a million subscribers and generated annual sales in excess of $150 million. Based on that trajectory, it went on to raise an additional $100 million from investors in Silicon Valley. It's one of the most exciting investments I've made and it's been fun to partner with people I like and respect on a business that is so innovative. It also made my time at Real Influence far more fruitful than I could ever have imagined. Given the growth of the company, the value of my shares has increased dramatically, so it turns out that my weekend at Playlist Live was time very well spent after all.

Choosing the Right Opportunities: The 10% Investment Process

Now that you know how to leverage your intellectual capital in order to determine what kinds of projects will play to your strengths, you can begin looking for opportunities. At this point, you're probably asking yourself: How do I find projects that are relevant to me? You might even have a few ideas, but question how you'll know whether your idea is actually a *good* idea. That's where having an investment process makes a difference. It will help you think clearly and avoid the temptation to follow others or make decisions that are not in your best interests. Even though you will rely on lots of people in your work, you are the ultimate decision maker. The buck stops with you.

About a decade ago, I had the chance to observe the migration of the wildebeest in the Serengeti. The migration embodies the ultimate lesson in followership. By the hundreds of thousands, wildebeest trail one another across the desert. They move quickly, forming a serpentine caravan over the plain and they are packed together so closely that there is no space between the tail of one animal and the horns of the next. Periodically, when the group comes to a stop, the animals gather in tight clusters before recommencing their journey. As the herd advances toward its destination, you begin to see the deeper meaning behind this seemingly endless parade. It's a survival strategy based on swarm intelligence. Moving as a group makes it difficult for predators to hunt more than a few members at a time, so even if a lion or crocodile picks off one animal or another, the vast majority of the group moves forward, blissfully unaware that their comrade has fallen.

Don't be a wildebeest. Hiding in the swarm cannot save you from making a bad investment—it only ensures that you will lose your money along with a bunch of other people. As a 10% Entrepreneur, you are not simply going to go with the flow or accept things as they seem on the surface. You will frequently collaborate with others, but whether you are evaluating your first or your thirty-first opportunity, you must avoid the temptation to merely follow someone else's lead. I've seen more than a few supposedly "experienced" investors describe their entire rationale for an investment in the following terms: "[Brand name venture capital firm] is investing." I'm going to call foul on that strategy. To me, that's like copying someone else's homework—you don't learn a thing and you have no idea if their answers are correct in the first place. The clearest path to becoming an experienced and savvy investor is to learn by doing. If you skip the "doing" part of the process and instead make decisions based on the actions of others, you're bound to make mistakes and then repeat them over and over again. Whenever I encounter an investment strategy that is predicated on followership, I'm always tempted to ask, "If [brand name venture capital firm] jumped off a bridge, would you jump, too?"

That begs the question: aren't there plenty of examples of venture capitalists that could be considered wildebeest? Of course. Some investors just chase trends and follow other firms, but there's a big difference between those people and you: they are playing with other people's money, while you are not. You are committing your own resources, whether in the form of time, financial capital, or both. That means that if you cut corners or follow others, you could be the one jumping off a bridge. Last time I checked, wildebeest don't fly.

Once you're in business, you're going to find yourself evaluating lots of new opportunities that come your way. Integrating entrepreneurship into your career is about more than balancing risk and reward. It is also about choosing a radically different mind-set from that of being an "employee." All of a sudden, you have total control over which opportunities you will and will not pursue. There is now a direct link between effort and potential return without needing to worry about corporate policy or the myriad other factors that dilute rewards in a corporate setting. You will also never know where each project will take you. Today's Real Influence might be tomorrow's ipsy.

At the same time, even the mere prospect of getting started can be a little overwhelming. It was for me. Autonomy sounds amazing on paper. It's great to have options, but it's also a responsibility. When you have the ability to make choices, then you have to actually *make choices*. You cannot duck behind others when you exhibit poor judgment or don't know quite what to do.

For all the psychic value that comes with freedom, it can be intimidating. Counting on your personal efforts and effectiveness to generate rewards is both logical and appealing, but there is also a loss of security. You can no longer skate along and get paid irrespective of your success on a given day.

Having a clear methodology, known as an investment process, will allow you to apply the step-by-step process that selective and experienced venture capitalists follow when they make investments. Thinking like a venture capitalist will save you time, help you to think with rigor, and teach you to see patterns and learn as you go along. It will also give you confidence that you're making decisions based on the facts and your intellectual capital rather than momentum or emotion. When you make a commitment, you will know that you've done your homework. The five-step process, shown below, is critically important and it cannot be outsourced to anyone.

The 10% Investment Process

SOURCING	SCREENING	DUE DILIGENCE	FINAL DECISION	DOCUMENTATION
Find the Opportunity	Assess How It Fits Your 10% Plan	Analyze the Opportunity	Commit or Pass	Make It Official

The first step is sourcing, whereby you will generate a pipeline of opportunities that could be promising candidates for your 10%. From this pipeline, you will employ a screening process to eliminate those ventures that don't fit the parameters of your 10% Plan. Next, you will undertake due diligence in order to evaluate the overall attractiveness of each opportunity. Based on your findings, you will make a final decision and decide to either move forward or to pass. Finally, you will make everything official by formalizing your involvement through proper legal documentation.

1. Sourcing

Thanks to your work so far, when you sit down at your laptop on your first day of work as a 10% Entrepreneur, you'll have a good sense of the resources you can bring to bear. You'll also have a feeling for the kinds of 10% projects that you're going to pursue, at least at the outset. What will you do next? After the initial rush that comes with starting something has passed, you have to figure out how to actually *start*. You will want to make your first investment, meet your first partner, or come up with an idea so compelling that you are certain that it's the highest and best use of your time. Those are all good impulses. You're going to need to simultaneously hustle and focus, so a sense of urgency can work in your favor. Still, you need to balance this enthusiasm with patience. You're not here to plant a seed as quickly as possible in the hope that something grows. You are here to build a garden that will be around for years to come.

When it comes to sourcing that first project, Michael Mayes, a Los Angeles–based 110% Entrepreneur, borrows a term from the real estate world to capture how you can get started: you need an anchor tenant. Imagine you're developing a real estate project, say an office building or shopping mall. The first tenant you get in the building—known as the anchor tenant—puts you in business and takes some pressure off. You don't have to lose sleep because you know that you've got a paying tenant signed up. The anchor tenant also says something to the world and sets the tone for everything that is to come. It provides a halo effect, telling people that you're in business, and helping to attract new tenants. If you pick the right anchor tenant, everything else can come together.

Your anchor tenant is the person or opportunity that gets you started. For me, joining forces with Marcelo on Real Influence was that anchor tenant. I knew him from earlier in my career and I called him when I was looking for an opportunity to work on something new. I also trusted him, and saw the opportunity as an adventure and a way to learn. There was little at risk (just my pride), but I also really cared about doing well and making an impact because I respected him and wanted to help him succeed. With my anchor tenant in place, I learned how to be a 10% Entrepreneur as I networked to build a pipeline of business for Real Influence, pitched potential clients, and reached out to anyone in my network who could be interested in the service. More important, having a real Advisor role was almost like hanging an "Open for Business" sign around my neck and on my LinkedIn profile.

Once you do find an initial project, you won't stop. As you will see in the next chapter, sourcing is a networking activity in many ways. As you build your pipeline, you'll keep an ear to the ground and continue talking to people, all the while generating a universe of potential projects that you will feed into your investment process, narrowing your focus at each stage until only the best candidates remain. At this point, don't worry too much about how many projects you have on your plate. Your goal is to invest your time as wisely as possible, so you are going to reduce the field during the next phase of your investment process. When you're sourcing, the bigger and better the universe, the greater your chance of finding something truly extraordinary. That said, if you find that you're too busy to evaluate and respond to potential opportunities in a timely manner, it's time to slow down for a while. You don't want to alienate the people who bring you deals by being unresponsive or unreliable.

2. Screening

Once you've got one or more opportunities in hand, your next step is to figure out if any of them match your objectives and resources. Based on the work you did earlier in this book, you will determine whether they fit the criteria you formulated for your 10% Plan. This is referred to as screening, and it's the first step in narrowing down your pipeline. To do so, you will think about how an opportunity aligns with your resources, namely your time and you financial and intellectual capital. You're basically asking yourself two questions:

- Do I have the resources to successfully include this in my 10%?
- Do I want to include this in my 10%?

In the screening phase, your aim is to be ruthlessly efficient. The average venture capitalist invests in a small percentage of the projects that come across his desk, so it pays to be picky. You don't want to waste time on things that don't fit your criteria. If it doesn't match your resources, you don't know the people who are going to be your partners, or you aren't playing to your strengths, then the deal just isn't for you. Based on those factors alone, I usually eliminate more than half of the deals in my pipeline right away. A lot of the time, I find myself remembering that I'm a 10% Entrepreneur and not a wildebeest. It's tempting to invest with friends even though you don't really understand how a restaurant operates or an app makes money. You can fall in love with an idea or a team, but if their business doesn't play to your strengths, your time is best spent elsewhere. If you screen out these situations early on, you save yourself from coming to the same realization when you embark on due diligence, which is a far more detailed process.

By quickly cutting down the field, you can instead spend your time focusing on the universe of projects that are worthy of an investment of time and brainpower. When you pass up an opportunity, just make sure to respond quickly, say thank you, and explain that although the opportunity may be very compelling for someone else, it doesn't match your skills and your interests. No one will fault you for saying "No, thank you," but they will fault you if you're unresponsive or you waste their time. That said, as you screen, you will learn about all kinds of businesses and meet a constant stream of new people who can help you to source even more deals once they better understand your criteria. So while you're going to be passing on much of what you see without spending a lot of time on the details, your horizons and your network will naturally broaden.

Once you're up and running, you'll find that the screening process is usually pretty straightforward. You'll start to recognize patterns and concentrate your efforts on the types of ventures that best fit your 10% Plan. In the beginning, however, when you're looking for your anchor tenant, Michael Mayes, whom you met earlier in this chapter, suggests sticking to one hard-and-fast rule: Pick something that "doesn't make you freak out." Michael is no stranger to leveraging his existing skills and relationships to invest in new areas. He's shifted deftly between working in the corporate sector, launching his own side ventures, and starting his own firm. As a first-time entrepreneur, you're already operating outside of your comfort zone, he says, so pick an area that you understand, that is "close to home," and that integrates into the rest of your life. That will ensure that you know what you're doing, have the intellectual capital to make it work, and actually enjoy the experience. In essence, you'll be playing to your strengths. Once you've got your bearings, you can widen your focus and expand into related areas of expertise.

Having Real Influence as my anchor tenant positioned me to move quickly and with confidence when the ipsy opportunity crossed my desk. I knew from my time working with Marcelo that he was at the forefront of an emerging industry that had the potential to generate millions or billions of dollars in value. I also knew that he was highly committed and that he had the skills and the relationships to make a real run at building a sizeable business. Still, while this was exactly the kind of project that played to my strengths, my work wasn't done. I knew my potential partner well and understood the industry, but I wasn't going to base my decision on emotion or just trust my gut.

3. Due Diligence

If an opportunity makes it past screening, the real work begins—you will initiate due diligence. Due diligence is the process of doing your homework—turning over all the stones and making sure that there are no surprises. This is the part of the investment process where you will think like a venture capitalist—one who isn't a wildebeest—to analyze the business rationale of an opportunity.

Enthusiasm for a project is good, and you shouldn't move forward without it, but while it's necessary, it's not sufficient. The worst thing any entrepreneur—from 10% through to 110%—can do is fall in love with an idea. If you fall in love, you might not ask the tough questions, think with a cool head, or allow yourself to say no if you don't have conviction in the business or the team. First and foremost, your goal as a 10% Entrepreneur is to make intelligent business decisions. The good news is that most due diligence comes down to a combination of common sense and attention to detail. You will assess the quality of the business, the team, and all the components of the opportunity. You will make sure that the story adds up, that the team doesn't shy away from tough questions, and that you can substantiate the business case with facts and data.

Over the course of my career, I've invested in more than twenty businesses and analyzed hundreds more. These companies have ranged from Silicon Valley–based startups to larger, more established firms operating in the United States, Latin America, and Asia. Suffice it to say that I've seen my share of due diligence over the years. While it would be logical to assume that the due diligence process varies radically depending on the type of company involved, I've learned that it's a surprisingly standard process. That's good news because it means that you'll learn and improve as you go along. No matter where a company is located, what it does, or where it is in its growth cycle, the diligence process comes down to a few universal questions:

1. Is this business positioned for success, and does it operate in an attractive industry? Will your return on investment compensate for the risks?
2. Are your partners, from the investors to the managers, competent and ethical? Are all parties' incentives properly aligned?

Those two points are sufficient for most investors, but as a 10% Entrepreneur, you will add one more set of criteria to the list:

3. Will this venture fit within your 10% Plan so that you can (i) contribute meaningfully to the company, and (ii) make connections or gain experience and intellectual capital for future endeavors?

That's it. If you can answer each of those questions in the affirmative, then you've done your work and followed your investment process. You are now ready to become an Angel, or an Advisor, or to file your articles of incorporation and become a Founder.

So how do you answer these questions? It all comes down to doing your homework. You will gather data, ask many more probing questions—including of yourself—and then synthesize your thinking based on what you learn. You'll never have perfect information and there will be some gray areas, so you will need to exercise informed reasoning along the way. You will also be a skeptic. Throughout the entire due diligence process, you will think and act independently, based on your own analyses and assessments. Applying rigor to your thinking will help you to avoid the temptation to rush, take the easy road, or follow someone else.

It's worth noting that your work will vary depending on your role. If you're an Angel or Advisor, due diligence allows you to assess whether you think someone else's business is positioned for success. In contrast, if you're a Founder, you will focus less on assessing the work and potential of others, and will instead evaluate your own ideas. You will validate the market, develop your business model, and gauge your ability to drive the idea forward. This analysis will eventually become the backbone of your business plan, a document that you prepare not only for yourself, but also for potential investors or partners.

No matter what kind of business venture you're evaluating, you will focus your time and attention on the same three topics:

1. The Business
2. Your Partners
3. Your Role

The Business

Is this business positioned for success, and does it operate in an attractive industry? Will your return on investment compensate for the risks?

All facts are friendly and due diligence is a process that uncovers facts. Almost without exception, I've found that my worst investments were the ones I made when I didn't truly understand a deal. By following your investment process, you'll avoid the temptation to get involved in those types of projects. During the screening phase, you weeded out anything that was too far afield from your base of knowledge for you to be able to conduct due diligence. Now your work begins. During diligence you are putting together the pieces of a puzzle. If you are playing to your strengths, you can fill in the first pieces of the puzzle relatively quickly, which will make it that much easier to see if the big picture makes sense. It will also help you to figure out whom to call if you need advice, information, or a second opinion. With ipsy, I was able to analyze the business and see the opportunity from a privileged position. I understood the business model, knew the CEO, and believed in the market. That made due diligence easier, and it also allowed me to ask smarter questions and better assess the risks and the potential returns.

Here are the critical questions about the business that you should be asking at this stage of due diligence:

Due Diligence Checklist: The Business

- Who is going to be managing the business? Why are these people positioned for success?
- What are the drivers of success and failure for this company? How will it make money? Who are its customers?
- What are the competitive dynamics in this industry? What is the size of the market? How can the company gain and defend market share?
- What are the key risks? What could cause it to fail, and how likely is such a scenario?
- What will this business and industry look like in three to five years? What does success look like?
- What kind of talent will the company need to attract to be successful?
- Does the company adequately protect its intellectual property, if necessary?
- What has been the financial and operational performance of the company to date? How achievable are its growth projections?
- How much capital will be required for this business? What are the sources of capital?
- Will you be able to invest more if the business is successful? Will you be expected to invest more?

- What will be the form of your investment? What will be offered in exchange for your investment of time, money, or a combination of the two?
- What is the time horizon for this investment? When can you expect to see returns?
- What are the potential financial returns for this investment under various scenarios?
- Will the founders or other shareholders of the company make money before you do? Is the upside fairly distributed between founders, management, and investors?

In order to get to the bottom of these questions, you will rely on your own knowledge, the knowledge that resides in your network (we'll talk about that in detail in the next chapter), and good old-fashioned hard work. I like to think of conducting due diligence as akin to writing a term paper. You can draw from nearly infinite sources, so it's your job to gather information, place it into context, and develop your own viewpoint. In fact, many people choose to structure their due diligence findings in the form of a report or a memo that collects all their insights, questions, and ideas in one document.

You'll want to get organized because you're going learn a great deal during due diligence. As you proceed, you will meet with members of the management team, pose questions, and then work to independently confirm any areas of doubt with your own legwork. You will take notes, synthesize your thoughts, and keep track of data you'd like to see while jotting down any questions that come to light as you learn.

As you've observed with the 10% Entrepreneurs in this book, success is all about figuring out how to answer the questions you have about a business. In order to assess demand and validate the market, Gabe Haim of Oyster Bay Brewing Company spent his weekends driving around Long Island studying the competition, while Dipali Patwa of Masala Baby attended a baby-clothing trade show. Everyone you've met in this book, from the guys at Monday Night Brewing and Silvercar to Luke Holden of Luke's Lobsters and Diego Saez-Gil of Bluesmart, put together a memo or a business plan that asked and then answered all the things they needed to know about the business. It's a process that requires an investment of time, but at the end of your work, which can take anywhere from a few weeks to a few months or more, you will have developed a view on the potential of the business. You will also have contemplated areas of risk while asking yourself why this business could potentially fail. All this knowledge will make you a better and more informed investor and will allow you to pitch in more effectively once you've sealed the deal.

One of the most enjoyable aspects of due diligence is the opportunity to meet new people and get out into the world. You can think of every due diligence meeting as a chance to connect with the person across the table, learn something about their business, and build a basic level of trust in what might become a meaningful relationship. You can also see due diligence as a way to break out of the cubicle and observe business in the real world. If you're thinking about investing in a restaurant or a store, go spend a few hours observing the comings and goings and talking to customers. Try the products and experience the company's offerings for yourself. Until you've driven a Silvercar, dressed your children in Masala Baby tunics, traveled with a Bluesmart suitcase, or tried one of Luke's lobster rolls, you haven't experienced the joy that lies at the end of all the hard work.

After you've completed your homework, you can then assess

whether you think the opportunity is attractive when compared to the risks. If you're backing a very early-stage venture where the execution risk is high, you want to believe that you could make an attractive return, say five times or ten times your money or even more if the company is successful. Now consider how you'd feel if you invested in a high-risk venture and you got only your money back with a small return, while the founders walked away with millions. You took lots of risk, but the founders got all the upside. On the other hand, you would not expect to make ten times your cash on more established and stable investments with lower risk. During due diligence, you will want to sit with the founders of the company to understand the return they envision for you and to find out their expectations for themselves. If you are the Founder, make sure the upside potential justifies your investment of resources. You can then judge whether you think that return is sufficient for the risk profile of the business. If it is, you can move on to evaluating your partners.

Your Partners

Are your partners, from the investors to the managers, competent and ethical? Are all parties' incentives properly aligned?

The probability of success and your overall enjoyment will be directly correlated to how carefully you select your partners, so you'll want to work with people who share your goals and values. That's nonnegotiable. These are the people who are going to make it possible for you to take part in an entrepreneurial venture even though you're holding down a day job. You want to be confident that they are going to protect your interests alongside theirs, respect your role in the business, act with the highest level of integrity, and make money for you and with you.

Just as enthusiasm for the business is necessary, enthusiasm for your partners is as well. Entrepreneurship is rewarding when you work with people who inspire you. But enjoying your partners' company is not enough. Evaluating a partner isn't just about deciding that you like a person. The failure of most businesses comes down to a failure of people, and lots of very nice people fail. If a company has weak management or hires the wrong mix of people, there will be missed opportunities and errors in judgment.

Scott Foushee, one of my mentors in the investment business, always told me that a bad partner is "the gift that keeps on giving." If you make a mistake and choose the wrong partner, you might find yourself on the receiving end of that unwelcome gift. One unfortunate choice not only dooms an investment, but it can also put your reputation at risk. Remember, your name is on the share certificate or the list of Advisors, and you may very well be on the hook for the actions of your partners. If there are problems, especially issues that involve a lapse in ethical judgment, you may someday find your name right next to theirs on the front page of the business section. As my mother always told me, "If you lie down with dogs, you get up with fleas." Fortunately, the opposite is also true. If you surround yourself with people like Marcelo, Michelle, and Nir, all of whom got me excited about ipsy, you will learn, have fun, and share in the excitement of building a real company.

So how do you figure out whether you're working with the right partners? During the screening process, you weeded out ventures if you didn't know the people involved. Still, just because you know someone doesn't mean you shouldn't ask hard questions. When assessing your potential partners, follow the checklist on page 135 to ensure that you are on the right track. Your diligence should encompass key managers, investors, and any other major stakeholders in the company who will also be your partners.

Due Diligence Checklist: Your Partners

- How will each significant person drive the business forward? Does each person have what it takes to succeed?
- Has this person been successful before in a relevant or related endeavor? Does the team have a track record?
- Does this person share your professional ethics?
- Where are the holes in the team?
- Has this person been through conflicts with business partners or employers?
- Is this person open about his past experiences, both successes and failures?
- Is this person willing to accept advice, feedback, and criticism?
- Are there any conflicts of interest?
- Will this person share information and keep you advised of key developments?
- Does this person value your contribution? Will he pick up the phone when you call?
- Do the founders of the business have meaningful "skin in the game"? Have they made a significant investment in terms of time, money, or both?
- Do the founders and managers have appropriate incentives (i.e., ownership in the company) to keep them focused and committed?

- Who are the other Angels, Advisors, and investors in the venture? Why are they involved, and how do they view the opportunity? Has the company attracted "smart money"?

With direct acquaintances, you can rely on prior interactions, along with the prior questions, to feel confident that you've done your homework. When it comes to the people you do not know, you will need to summon your inner Sherlock Holmes. In addition to asking the previous questions, I like to use LinkedIn and other social networks to find someone who has relevant knowledge on the subject. I then speak to these sources to make sure there are no hidden issues and to confirm the quality of the team.

Most people are refreshingly candid. If they respect an entrepreneur and a team, they will sing their praises. If they've been burned, they will go out of their way to make sure that doesn't happen again to someone else. On more than one occasion, I've turned up some critical information through a mutual contact that's convinced me to pass on a deal. If you find that you are still not sure, or you don't feel you have a strong enough network to get the information you need, you can also request a few references. If someone is unwilling to provide you with a list of professional references, then he's probably not the kind of person you want as a partner. It's a huge red flag. As a last gut check, I make sure to spend some time on Google investigating the team. You'd be surprised by how much you can learn online, so even though relying on Google is not sufficient on its own, it's still a worthy exercise.

Finding the right partner requires patience, but the result can be a game changer. Luke Holden knew he needed help in order to open and manage stores while holding down his job in finance. Like any millennial, he took his search to Craigslist and posted an ad. He then combed through a stack of six hundred resumés and seriously considered ten candidates before meeting Ben Conniff. Ben had a background in the food industry and was passionate about Luke's Lobster from day one. They each took a leap of faith, but even in their wildest dreams, they could never have imagined they'd have found such success together.

No matter how smart or talented you are as an Angel or Founder, you never have all the resources you're going to require to achieve your goals. You will need to find ways to address gaps in knowledge or skills. Your partners represent an investment in the future: over time, as you build a reputation and a series of relationships, the people part of the business gets far easier. Once you have a group of trusted partners, they will serve as a source of new ideas and opportunities. They will become part of your machine and they will help to make everything work better. When I think about my own 10%, relationships—more than anything else   made it all possible.

Your Role

> *Will this venture fit within your 10% Plan so that you can (i) contribute meaningfully to the company, and (ii) make connections or gain experience and intellectual capital for future endeavors?*

In your 10%, you will be way too excited and engaged in your side ventures to want to run on autopilot. You're here because you wish to learn, make new connections, and build something for yourself. Enough watching from the sidelines—this is your chance to suit up and play!

No matter what role I take in a venture, I usually find I want to do more than just write a check. I can only get really excited about situations in which I believe I can directly add value. When you're a 10% Entrepreneur, you want to know that you can provide advice, make connections, or contribute to solving one of the dozens of challenges that companies tackle on a daily basis, so that your involvement will make the company more valuable. Your rationale for this approach is based on three factors, all of which are driven by self-interest. First, if you can't move the needle in some way to increase a company's chance of success, it's fair to question whether you know enough about its business. Second, if you can't help the team, how will you build a meaningful relationship that can lead to future opportunities? How will you plant more seeds in the future? Third, taking an active role allows you to build a track record and a reputation. If you were content with being an observer, you could trade stocks instead.

Before becoming an Angel or an Advisor at a company, spend time with the management team to understand why they want you to be part of their company. If you decide to work together, you will be building a partnership that will ideally span years, so you should understand what they believe you can contribute. Do they need help with financing, connections, advice, or a mix of all sorts of things? How much time should you dedicate to helping them? The same holds true for Founders and their business partners. If you're going to start a company with new partners, you will want to spend time with each member of your team in order to make sure you are on the same page with respect to what each person will bring to the table. I've known several entrepreneurs who gave away a meaningful share of their company to a partner who ended up doing very little. One of these absentee partners sold his stake for more than $1 million without having done anything to deserve that kind of payday!

Tackling these issues early on is essential to setting expectations and to clarifying how each person in the business sees her role going forward. Once you strip away all the products, numbers, and contracts, every business is about people, and these issues can be very personal in nature. You may find yourself talking about subjects, perhaps money, that are uncomfortable or even a little awkward. Awkward is actually good. A little tension now will save misunderstandings in the long run, and it's better to learn at the beginning that you have widely diverging views than when you're sitting down to sign a contract. Plus, you want a sense of how your possible partners behave when things get real. As you've seen, Founders may have distinct interests and different paths in mind. Peter Barlow never contemplated leaving his law firm for Silvercar, and only two of the three Founders of Monday Night Brewing opted to join the company full time. These issues, while easily addressable, cannot be ignored as you plan for growth.[1]

Getting to know a management team and then discussing how you can add tangible value to the endeavor makes everything far more meaningful. As an Advisor, I like to caucus with the CEO and set a list of expectations for each party on a periodic basis. Having that conversation ensures that I'm spending my time in a way that truly helps the team while also validating that the CEO and other key managers will use my time wisely. The more impactful you are as an Angel or Advisor, the better. This is not only going to increase the value of your investments, it will deepen your relationships with the people in your 10%. It will also allow you to demonstrate your value to all the other people around the table. Ideally, they will be your partners in many future endeavors, and the greater your impact, the more they will want to work with you.

I was an investor in Diego Saez-Gil's first company, WeHostels. When he was selling the company to a strategic investor, he called me often for advice. We'd get together, pore over spreadsheets, and analyze the terms of the deal and the implications of the transaction for the investors and management. This was Diego's first time selling a company, so I was happy to draw on my experience dealing with similar situations. The high-stakes negotiations during the sale process allowed us to get to know each other while building a good deal of trust during those conversations. After he sold the company, Diego didn't forget the time we spent working together. When he joined Bluesmart as a 110% Entrepreneur, he offered me the opportunity to be both an Angel and an Advisor from the outset.

In order to position yourself for success, you can use the questions below to assess your potential role in each venture:

Due Diligence Checklist: Your Role

- How do your resources map to the needs of the company both today and in the future?
- Do you have intellectual capital and relationships that will allow you to contribute meaningfully to the success of the venture?
- Does the management team value your input and ideas? Will they want to engage with you and seek your advice?
- Do you feel comfortable with the team? Are you able to have straightforward conversations based on facts and data, rather than emotion?

- Is the company responsive to your requests? Do they provide information and answer questions in a timely manner?
- What can you learn in this venture that will make you a better 10% Entrepreneur?
- Will you be able to form relationships that will help you to grow your 10%?
- If you're an Advisor, does the company set specific objectives and expectations with regard to your role?
- If you're a Founder, are your partners ready to commit? Are all parties prepared to sign agreements with respect to each person's specific level of involvement and economic stake?

4. Final Decision

Once you have completed due diligence, you are ready to decide whether you are going to move forward. It's at this point that you make a final decision. When venture capital firms make investment decisions, the investment committee gets together to hash out the merits and risks of the deal. Based on that discussion, they take a vote. If you're not quite sure, or you just want a second opinion, you might find it helpful to consult with friends or family in order to talk through any lingering doubts. It's like having your own ad hoc investment committee. Once you've made up your mind, you can move forward with your final decision. If you are satisfied with your due diligence findings and you believe that the opportunity fits with your strategy, it's time to say yes. If it doesn't meet all of your expectations, then you'll politely pass. Sometimes the best investment decisions you'll ever make are the ones when you say no.

It's always a little scary to settle on that final decision and decide to move forward and make an investment. That's particularly true when you're an Angel, since you're investing your hard-earned money. When I was investing in ipsy, I did my diligence and thought carefully about the team and my level of involvement in the company. By following an investment process, I had sufficient information to make a final decision. Nonetheless, I was nervous. In the end, I realized that since I didn't have a crystal ball, I needed to trust my due diligence. If I couldn't get comfortable investing in such a compelling business and partnering with people I knew well, then I'd probably never invest in anything.

When you're making your final decision, you will once again return to the questions that framed the entire due diligence process:

Final Decision Checklist

- Is this business positioned for success?
- Can you achieve an attractive return on your investment?
- Are your partners competent and ethical?
- Are all parties' incentives properly aligned?
- Can you contribute something meaningful to the company's success?
- Can you make connections or develop intellectual capital that will have future benefits?

Always keep in mind that this is a process and that you'll learn, improve, and even make a few mistakes. As you gain experience, you will see a wider range of opportunities and meet new people. Even if you decide to pass, you never know what may happen in the future. Entrepreneurs learn, too, and the person whose idea is not quite right today might have a blockbuster business up her sleeve for the next time around. So if you're passing, you can still view this interaction as a chance to keep in touch for the future. There is no good reason to burn bridges. You want to leave every potential partner with a favorable impression of your intellect and your ethics, whether you become partners or not. You can do this by making decisions quickly and sticking to them. You never want to string someone along. They are working hard to build a business and they are counting on you to respect their time. Plus, by acting in a timely manner, you'll free up capacity and resources in order to move on to the next opportunity.

5. Documentation

Since smart business people always make sure to get things in writing, once you've decided to move ahead, it's time for the documentation phase. The specific documents required will depend on your role:

1. If you're an Angel, you'll need to sign contracts in which you buy shares in a company.
2. If you're an Advisor, you will negotiate and sign an Advisor agreement in which you agree to a minimum level of commitment in exchange for shares.
3. If you're a Founder, you will document your arrangement with your investors and partners.
4. If you're an Aficionado or a 110% Entrepreneur, you will follow the same steps as the Angel, the Advisor, or the Founder, based on the nature of your involvement.

Depending on your professional background, you may already be comfortable dealing with the types of discussions, negotiations, and legal documents that will be a part of this stage of the investment process. If you are not, there's no need to worry. The legal side of entrepreneurship is less complicated than you might imagine or, for many people, fear. If you haven't had much experience with contracts, the first time you read through a legal document might be a little intimidating, but over time you'll notice that many agreements use similar formats and terminology.[2] Also, given the fact that most small companies cannot sink large sums of cash into paying lawyers, there has been a movement to simplify and standardize the basic legal documents required in a transaction.[3] That said, you, and perhaps someone whose judgment you trust, should carefully read through all of the documents and surface any questions.

Avoid the temptation to settle if you aren't sure that your understanding of the deal is consistent with the contract. Ask questions of the company's management, its lawyers, or anyone else who can help you understand the terms. It's in everybody's interest to make sure that you're comfortable with all the agreements. Entrepreneurs want their partners to be happy, after all. That said, negotiating to death or dragging your feet doesn't serve anyone's purposes. The ipsy fund-raising involved a lead investor who negotiated a set of terms on behalf of all the investors in the round. Since I was a smaller investor, I was expected to accept these terms as well. Once I read the documents and confirmed that they reflected my understanding of the transaction, I signed them. It would be impractical and expensive for each small investor to try to negotiate his own distinct agreement.

If you're really worried or unsure about where to begin, you can always join an angel investment group. As you'll see in the next chapter, investing as part of a group will give you the confidence and resources you need to learn so that you can work more independently in the future. You may also want to consider working with legal counsel and an accountant in order to get advice for more complex situations or when you feel uncertain. This small up-front investment could avoid headaches later on. That said, lawyers are often willing to give a little free advice to friends or people who are in their networks, with the idea that in the future you will find ways to introduce them to clients, such as the companies in your 10%.

When all is said and done, the investment process is the linchpin of your work as a 10% Entrepreneur. It's also the part of your 10% Plan that will serve as a bridge between your resources and the resources of all the people in your network. By drawing upon the talents of others, you will make each step of your investment process, from sourcing straight through to documentation, more effective. As you will see in the next chapter, your network will make your efforts count for more than the hours, money, or ideas that you could ever contribute on your own.

Chapter 8

Building Your Team

I f you're going to make it as a 10% Entrepreneur, you're not going to do it alone. Since you're investing just a portion of your
resources into entrepreneurial ventures, and you're doing so in
a part time capacity, you will need to collaborate with other
people who can help to make each of your assets count for much
more. That's where teamwork comes into the picture. It's the last
step in formulating your 10% Plan. You will be drawing on your
network in order to surround yourself with a community of
people who will contribute to and benefit from everything you're
building. As a result, your enterprise will be highly scalable.

Surrounding yourself with the right people makes a difference in most places, but it's mission critical in China. William
Bao Bean should know. William sits on the steering committee
of AngelVest, China's largest angel investment group. Since
2007, the group has evaluated over a thousand companies, backing more than thirty of them. When it comes to investing in

entrepreneurial ventures, China can feel a bit like the Wild West, but if you know what you're doing, opportunity abounds. That's where AngelVest comes into the picture. Its members are a diverse group of people who spend their days working in real estate, marketing, finance, technology, health care, law, and at large industrial companies. They are also all 10% Entrepreneurs who band together as Angels to make investments.

The beauty of joining an angel group, whether you're in Beijing, Berlin, or Boston, is that you will benefit from the combined wisdom and experience of like-minded individuals who share your goals. Even if you've never made an investment before, you can surround yourself with experienced investors who will take you under their wing and help you get started. At each stage of the investment process, AngelVest is structured to harness the talents of individuals for the benefit of the whole. Members scour the country to source the most promising new companies and then collaborate to conduct due diligence and supervise the investment process. Throughout, they are encouraged to learn from one another. Lawyers give pointers to people who work in marketing, technology entrepreneurs learn about real estate, and everyone comes out smarter and more connected.

Having the right people around you isn't just critical when you're investing in China, it's also instrumental to running a business there. Although he grew up in the United States, Gavin Newton-Tanzer is the founder of Sunrise International Education, which organizes English-language extracurricular programs for more than fifty thousand students. By offering afterschool education, such as English-language debate programs, Gavin provides the next generation of Chinese students with the language and critical-thinking skills they will need to study in the West.

As a twentysomething American starting a company in an industry where gray hair matters, Gavin knew he needed to surround himself with leading minds who could enhance his credibility on both sides of the Pacific. He resolved to recruit a group of Advisors, all 10% Entrepreneurs, including hard-hitting academics and well-known education industry executives. To attract the best people possible, Gavin crafted a strong pitch. These were busy people with lots of competing priorities, so when he approached them at conferences or via mutual contacts, he presented them with a detailed proposal of how he planned to work together. This specificity helped each prospective Advisor understand how Sunrise could fit into their priorities. Based on the results, it's clear that Gavin's pitch was compelling. He attracted a high-quality team of Advisors, including scholars in the United States and China; an executive at the Asia Society in New York; and a retired senior executive of Pearson, the world's largest education company.

Your team consists of all the people in your network with whom you will form long-term business relationships. In that sense, recruiting a team involves a lot more than just networking. It's about rallying people to your cause and getting them engaged alongside you. These relationships will be the fuel for your 10%. They will also make your experience fun, rewarding, and sustainable, serving as a constant in your life and your career that bridges you from one opportunity to the next. They are people you can trust who share your work ethic and will do right by you, as you will by them. Some will even become great friends. This chapter will show you how to assemble and collaborate with a team of people who can help in every aspect of your 10%, from sourcing and due diligence to taking an active role at the ventures in your portfolio.

Finding the Right Answer Is About Knowing Where to Look

When I was a kid, I was a grinder. My formula for academic success came down to a single input: hours. I firmly believed that if I studied harder than anyone else and devoted more time to preparation, I would always do well. That worked for a while, but by the time I'd made it to college, things were out of hand. Coming from a public high school in Maine, I was deathly afraid of doing poorly and wasting my parents' hard-earned money. My instincts told me to overprepare. During the first months of my freshman year, I somehow decided it would be wise to read the chapters of the textbooks that weren't assigned along with the ones that were. That ended up being my worst semester of school, mostly because I wasted time cramming my head with things that weren't even on the syllabus.

It wasn't until I spent my junior year abroad in Argentina that I finally chilled out. Argentines have a totally different—I'd say even socialist—approach to studying for exams. It was like attending college on a different planet, not just a different continent. Here's how it works. At the end of the semester, the person who took the best notes in the class makes a photocopy for everyone else. So although your final grade comes down to preparation, your intellect, and your performance the day of the test, all the materials you need to review are crowdsourced and shared freely. If you need anything, you just have to know whom to ask.

So much of business is about knowing the best person to contact in order to gather information that will allow you to make thoughtful decisions. You leverage your team and the smartest people you can find in order to get the data you need, make a decision, and keep moving. When you're a 10% Entrepreneur, working smart is just as important as working hard. You're not going to measure success by the number of hours you spend working. There is no such thing as face time, and you get zero credit and zero financial reward from toiling endlessly on your own. Rather, your success will correspond to how effectively you use your time. Knowing whom to call for help, advice, connections, or a second opinion will help you make time count for far more than the actual hours you spend on a project. Instead of reinventing the wheel, you will benefit from the years that someone else has spent amassing expertise for themselves.

When you lack intellectual capital in a certain area, you can draw on your network to fill in the gaps. Look below at the diagram of the 10% investment process, which you saw in the previous chapter. Here it's updated to reflect the ways in which you can leverage other people's knowledge and talents at each stage:

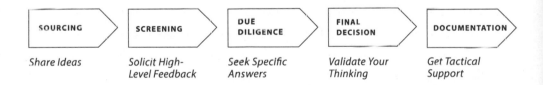

SOURCING	SCREENING	DUE DILIGENCE	FINAL DECISION	DOCUMENTATION
Share Ideas	Solicit High-Level Feedback	Seek Specific Answers	Validate Your Thinking	Get Tactical Support

So how does this all work in practice? As with a group like AngelVest, your network is fertile ground for sourcing. You can also ask around for quick feedback during screening to see if an opportunity meets your basic criteria. Once you get into due diligence, you will supplement your own homework with the expertise of others in order to fill in the missing pieces of the puzzle and unearth specific answers to the questions you encounter. As you make your final decision, you can seek advice from people who are willing to serve on your ad hoc investment committee and provide you with a gut check from time to time. Finally, if you need help on legal or other technical aspects of documentation, calling on an expert can be critical to saving time and making wise decisions. All these steps taken together amount to building your team.

As you can see, the investment process is about much more than grinding it out to find the information you need to make smart decisions. Your portfolio of activities will benefit immeasurably when you build a team and cultivate mutually beneficial relationships. Everything you're doing will be stronger and work better when you bring the right people into the mix. You'll also create a source of intellectual capital, opportunities, ideas, help, and future partners. This is a long-term undertaking, and once you've got the right people around you, you can find ways for these people to contribute to and then share in your success. In that way, giving advice and helping out is most definitely not a one-way street. You can find ways to help others just as they help you, thereby creating the conditions for a virtuous cycle. Each project in your 10% can also be part of someone else's 10%.

Your team will be radically different from other teams you've worked with in the past. There is no set roster and there is no established coach or boss. You will work together with great flexibility with the idea that in doing so you will generate a series of opportunities to cooperate, both now and in the future. This is not about winning quick points or making a fast dollar; it's about setting yourself up to have the resources you need for ongoing success. It's also about creating a community of people who will work with you and also work with one another. As a result, your network won't be hub and spoke in nature, requiring everything to go through you. Rather, your goal is to match like-minded people to each other so that they can collaborate, with you or even without you. In this sense, your team will be multipolar. Unlike a hub-and-spoke network, generating deals or sharing intellectual capital won't depend directly upon you.

One of the strengths of your team will be the way all the players work together, so the more connectivity you build among the people in your network, the better. As you link people with common interests, you will find that things will begin to take on a life of their own. The two people you introduced last week might end up becoming business partners next week. If they do end up working together, there's a good chance they'll invite you to join them. In that way, your network is up and running even when you're not.

Hub and Spoke Network   **10% Entrepreneur Network**

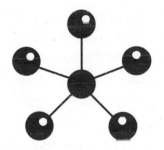 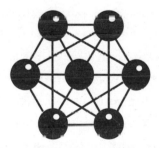

When I first connected Marcelo Camberos to Nir Liberboim, I did so in the context of Real Influence. Marcelo was looking for advice on how to pitch to cosmetics companies and Nir was knowledgeable about the sector. At that time, there was no immediate way for them to work together, but Nir was helpful and respectful of Marcelo's ideas. Nir couldn't have known it at the time, but this willingness to help was his ticket into a fantastic investment. Based on those initial interactions, Marcelo offered him the chance to become one of the first investors in ipsy. Imagine if Nir hadn't bothered to respond when I first introduced him to Marcelo. That would have been one very expensive mistake.

Of course, that means that 10% Entrepreneurs cannot just be takers. If you want smart people to pick up the phone each time you call them, you need to make it worth their while. It's not an issue of karma, it's about thinking for the long term. You may be asking for help today, but you will likely be giving it tomorrow. Engaging with people who can help you doesn't require you to ask them for much of their time, at least in the initial stages. You'll send some basic materials over to someone who knows the industry or the team and then ask them to give you feedback on the sector. You'll get the information you need, send a nice thank-you e-mail, and move on. People you know and trust will be willing to do favors for you, but over the long run, you can achieve even more by finding ways to bring them into your projects and then plugging them into your activities as one more connected pole within the entire system.

Now that you're thinking like someone who builds teams, you'll be surprised by how often you can find ways to collaborate with other smart and talented people. The more people you recruit to the movement, the better. Over time, things will start to hum and you'll be part of a living, breathing circle of people who are working on exciting projects. When you've built that machine and it's up and running, you'll be able to choose when, where, and how you want to be involved. Your career will reflect the diverse talents of the people on your team, and you will reap the benefits of their respective efforts, sometimes in unexpected ways. That's when it starts to get really fun. When your machine is multipolar, it doesn't depend on you alone to make things happen. You will be surprised by the network effects of all the work you do and you may find that you become an unexpected beneficiary.

A few years ago, I introduced a new acquaintance to my friend Suken Shah, who was starting an investment fund. I wasn't sure quite how they would work together, but my gut told me they would find some areas of common interest. Unbeknownst to me, they met a few weeks later at a Dunkin' Donuts, in what would become the first step to forming a full-fledged partnership. A year later, I got an e-mail from Suken with details of a company that they had decided to buy together. At the bottom of the e-mail, along with a thank-you, were details about the shares in the company that they'd given to me in appreciation for the introduction. When I got that e-mail, I realized that my 10% had taken on a life of its own. Without my even knowing it, my machine was working overtime.

Make Your Name the Most Important Brand on Your Business Card

Before you get to work assembling your team and building your machine, you need to get organized. You're going to be talking to a lot of people, so in order to make good use of everybody's time, you'll want to be able to clearly explain who you are and where you're going. Back in Chapter 6, you wrote a professional biography. What you may not have realized at the time was that you were actually conducting due diligence—on yourself. You were filling in the blanks and tying together everything in your career in a cohesive and understandable way. Now you can take this exercise to the next level and think about what it means to your brand and your offering.

You'll recall that when I was first starting my 10%, I did a horrible job of explaining myself. Before I got my story straight, I tended to rely on a rambling laundry list of activities and aspirations that confused just about everyone, including me. I learned through experience that the image you project to the world is very much how other people will see you. That's why you need a solid elevator pitch. If you can explain your expertise and what you're looking to do in a few sentences, you'll clear up the confusion and project confidence, credibility, and a sense of mission to the people around you. Going back to Gavin Newton-Tanzer, the young American entrepreneur operating in China, it's clear that he had his pitch down. He crafted customized messages for each potential Advisor that highlighted how he felt that individual would impact the success of his company. This came as a result of research, reflection, and lots of practice.

Creating your pitch will require some work in advance. Imagine you meet someone at a networking event and they ask you what you do for a living. This is your chance to tell them that you're a 10% Entrepreneur, so don't miss the opportunity. The good news is that thanks to your work back in Chapter 6, you already have all the basic components you need. The idea is to give people something they can latch on to, perhaps what you do at your day job or where you work, then bridge that to what you're looking to achieve. With some preparation, this can be surprisingly succinct. For example, Patrick Linnenbank's pitch can be summarized in just a few sentences:

I'm Patrick. I started my career as a doctor, but quickly decided I wanted to move to the business world. While working as a management consultant, I drew on my medical experience to train in forensics, especially in conflict zones. I became interested in security in areas of conflict, so I decided to bring it all together to form a security and forensics firm. I'm looking to grow into new regions if you know anyone good in the space.

Of course, he could also just say: "The name's Bond. James Bond." But then you'd never know he used to be a consultant.

The 10% Plan: Exercise 5—Crafting Your Pitch

Return to the shorter version of the biography that you crafted in Chapter 6. Using this biography as a base, develop a pitch. You only need a few sentences, but those sentences will include the following pieces of information:

- Your name
- What you "do"
- Why you are credible in that area (i.e., current or past experience)
- What you're looking to achieve in your 10%

The idea is to explain what you do by day, give some color on your 10%, and then perhaps mention any areas of focus where you're looking for help. Remember, you are giving a very high-level overview to invite further conversation.

> Once you have your pitch, think about how you can tailor it to different audiences, such as a potential business partner, a friend, someone who might show you investment opportunities, or a company you would like to join as an Advisor. The key to tailoring the pitch is to figure out the relevant "ask" for each audience. For example, if you're an Angel, you'll say, "I'm looking to invest in high-potential companies as an Angel." If you want to be an Advisor, you'll say, "I want to apply my knowledge and relationships as an Advisor." If you're seeking a business partner, you can also tailor the "ask" accordingly. Go ahead and be direct. With a quality pitch, you will have enough momentum to take a direct approach.

As you craft your pitch, you can experiment with how to integrate all the brands that you list on your resumé. This might include your university, past or present employers, and the names of the ventures in your 10%. For someone like Hillyer Jennings at Wrist Tunes, the link between his 10% and his alma mater is critical to the story, but for someone else it may not be as important. You can tailor all these factors to your audience, the situation, and what you find is working for you. In doing so, you'll find that one benefit of developing a tight pitch and learning to explain yourself is that people will generally want to know more. When your answer to "What do you do?" is longer than just a word or two, people tend to be intrigued. As long as you're clear and confident, you'll find that you'll soon be getting into the details. That's the first step to finding like-minded individuals as you begin to network.

Once you've got your pitch in good shape, practice until you project confidence and clarity. Also, practice with friends or mentors who can give you feedback.

Recruiting People to Your Team

Lots of people swear that networking is the number one driver of their success, but it's shocking how much time it can consume. As a recovering networking addict, I learned this lesson the hard way. I've spent countless hours having coffee, drinks, and meals, all in the name of networking. It's my own fault, since I genuinely like meeting new people and I believe that each and every interaction teaches me something. Yet for much of my career, and despite the sheer number of contacts in my orbit, I wasted a lot of time and energy in the process.

No one teaches us how to network. We learn slowly, over time, starting on the playground and advancing right through to professional mixers. We rarely stop to consider whether all this running around—the coffee chats, quick meetings, and industry-focused conferences—really amounts to anything. In general, there is far too much networking and not enough to show for it. Meeting as many people as possible seems reasonable when you're first starting out in your career or when you're in transition, but it's completely unsustainable when you're juggling lots of competing responsibilities. What's the point of collecting stacks of business cards if nothing ever comes of them?

Whether you're building your pipeline, looking for investors for a project, or seeking that anchor tenant, networking will be an important part of building the team of people who will help you get things done. While it's tempting to network tactically and cast about in multiple directions in search of a deal, you'll benefit far more from thinking systematically. If you can approach this exercise with rigor, you'll find that the return on your investment of time and energy will increase.

Start with your existing network. Your first stop will be your family and friends. They are the people who care most about you; you trust them and they will always be willing to help. Next, scour your address book and spend time on LinkedIn and other social media platforms. Then, return to the professional biography you prepared earlier and read it with the goal of creating a list of current or former colleagues, business contacts, or classmates who could be helpful. You want to be aware of anyone connected to your existing network who is doing something that seems exciting or interesting to you. Why should you put in all kinds of effort to meet new people when you might find just what you're looking for among the people you already know? After all, they will be the most responsive to your pitch.

Through in-person meetings, phone calls, or even while socializing at birthday parties or barbeques, you can activate your network and generate opportunities. The more you integrate these discussions into the rest of your life, the less friction they will create. During each of these conversations, ask for advice and introductions. This way, your growing contact base will be connected to people you know and trust. Keep track of these conversations and take notes so you have a record of the ideas and suggestions that come out of your interactions and can follow up from time to time. Also, don't forget that this isn't a selfish undertaking. Ask how you can help in return and start building your machine.

If you cannot find the right contacts through people you know and you need to communicate with individuals outside of your network, you are going to be entering cold-call territory. This could include approaching a speaker at a conference, getting in touch with an angel investment group, contacting the business accelerator at a local university, or calling someone you read about in a newspaper article. Cold calls can actually produce surprising results, depending on the industry and the context. Entrepreneurs are an especially open group of people, and most of them know what it's like to be asking others for help. This empathy means that they will tend to be responsive. If you're approaching someone with shared geographical, alumni, or professional ties, the chances are often better that you'll get a response. Even absent some shared ties, a well-constructed message and some follow through can be the keys to hearing back. I generally make time to meet with people who send me something compelling and are tenacious.

Whether you are cold-calling or reconnecting with an old friend or colleague, there are some basic points of etiquette and common sense that apply. Many people get dozens if not hundreds of e-mails a day and they don't want to read a note that has no point and no value—or what I like to call an "empty-calorie e-mail." When you're drafting any e-mail, cold call or otherwise, follow these guidelines:

- Use your personal e-mail
- Be cordial and succinct
- Personalize the text
- Never send a form letter
- Highlight any shared points of interest or mutual contacts
- Make a specific request—no one wants to trade endless messages to get to your "ask"
- Offer to help with anything they might need in return
- Always say please and thank you

- Follow up on outstanding items
- Be responsive
- Stay in touch and share news of future developments

Once you initiate contact, if you don't hear back within a week, try again or give them a call. Many busy people never answer the first e-mail they get asking for help. They respond to persistence rather than politeness. Of course, the line between asking for help and being a nuisance can get a bit blurry when you're in the heat of the moment. If someone doesn't get back to you after a few tries, then move on to the next person. They're either too busy to help you or they're not interested. Either way, they don't want to be on your team. Also, in the future, when you consider blowing somebody off in a similar fashion, think back to that moment.

Often, success in these types of endeavors is a direct result of being courteous when you're asking for help. If you're looking for a favor, make your request in a way that puts as little burden as possible on the person who is helping you. The easier you make it for people to help, the more likely they'll do so in a timely manner. For example, if you would like an introduction to one of their contacts, draft a succinct e-mail that provides some context for your request and includes any relevant materials. Draw upon your elevator pitch to make it clear that you mean business. Once you secure their assistance, send a separate, clean message for each person you want to meet. Make it as easy as possible for someone to forward your note along with any additional comments from their end. Also, if you want to make an introduction or connect two people who might have common interests, always ask before doing so. Making cold introductions can burn through goodwill very quickly and do even more damage than a barrage of empty-calorie e-mails.

Your efforts will take time to blossom and lead to tangible results. You are building a machine, so the more energy you invest into making it viable, the more it will thrive. This includes spending some time getting organized. For example, you can put together a database that will allow you keep track of your contacts and your interactions with the people in your 10%. This will require an up-front investment of time, but it will become a valuable tool that will support all of your efforts. Taking a systematic approach will make you more efficient and keep your machine humming. Every week, Peter Barlow of Silvercar drops short e-mails to five people in his network just to stay in touch. It's a system that he follows religiously and it keeps his relationships fresh.

Networking is all about putting yourself out there. If you're not sure where to start, you can meet scores of people in a short period of time by attending broad networking events. If you have your pitch ready, this may be worth your time, especially since events are often focused around specific professional interests. There are more than 200,000 Meetup groups with more than 22 million members operating in 180 countries, catering to any subject you can imagine.[1] They also represent just a fraction of the formal or informal networking events that you can find in your community. You will also have opportunities to use your pitch on a daily basis if you're prepared to make the effort. Whether you're at a dinner party, your kid's soccer game, or your college reunion, you can connect with people who might just be able to help. Plus, you can spare yourself from making small talk about the

The 10% Plan: Exercise 6—Building Your Team

Create a database of all the people who can help you and join your team. To do so, draw on the following types of resources:

- Your family and friends
- Your address book and database of contacts
- Your professional biography
- Social networks such as LinkedIn
- Your social group
- Business cards you've collected
- Alumni networks
- Professional networks
- Angel investment networks

weather and instead discuss something more substantial. You might even plant some seeds.

Import or enter these contacts into a database or a spreadsheet. Prioritizing among the people in your database, contact individuals who might be able to help you with your 10%. Set a goal of speaking to a minimum number of people per week, whether in person or over the phone. Keep notes on any discussions or interactions and flag contacts for follow-up as appropriate. Use this database on an ongoing basis in order to keep your network updated and organized. Consider adding specific details as you learn more about your contacts and their current activities. This could include information such as area of expertise, location, or industry focus. As you meet new people in other aspects of your life or contact individuals for your 10% via cold calls, add them to your database as well, noting how you might collaborate and flagging any follow-up items.

Seeking Specific Answers to Specific Questions

The power of your network doesn't stop at recruiting a group of team members. It also extends to due diligence and to pitching in to make the projects in your 10% more successful. You want to be confident in what you know and mindful of what you don't know. You're not afraid to ask questions because it's the unasked question that can make the difference between a good decision and a mistake. All facts are friendly and data trumps ego, so you're not looking for affirmation. Rather, your goal is to evaluate a set of opportunities that will be worth your time and resources. You will then determine how to integrate those opportunities into the rest of your life and your career. When you face unanswered questions, you will employ the same set of strategies you used for sourcing in order to build a team of people with functional expertise.

It is at this point that you are looking for specific answers to specific questions. You will do this by tapping into the intellectual capital of people who have more experience than you do in a given field. You will leverage your business judgment to gather data and evaluate the findings of your research, but you'll want the advice of people who are in a better position than you to make the call. For example, if you're looking to understand the seafood market in Manhattan, then you'll want to talk to Luke Holden. If you want to find out how investors look at that kind of retail business, then you'll find somebody like Farah Khan. Neither of these topics is unknowable, but they will require you to seek out people who can provide you with information, advice, and perspective as you conduct due diligence.

During due diligence, you leverage all the intellectual capital

165

and knowledge that resides in your network. Now that you have started to assemble your team, you will want to draw upon the collective wisdom of all these experts, since they possess insights and skills that you do not. One good phone call or coffee with an expert can save you time, point you in the right direction, or keep you out of trouble. Everything you learn can help you to ask the right questions and think through the business rationale of an opportunity, all the while equipping you with the tools you'll need to better understand the market, the product, and the prospects for success. Of course, you will be mindful to develop your own opinions, maintain a healthy level of skepticism, and generally avoid being a wildebeest, but you will be far the wiser for all these conversations.

You will also want to find people with particular talents who can help you later on, once you're formally involved in a business, either as an Advisor, an Angel, or a Founder. Now that you're a partner in a new endeavor, the real work begins, so knowing whom to call when you're looking for specific knowledge and skills is critical. Even as you build a network for sourcing and due diligence, you can also use this same community of people to find talented individuals who are able to engage in projects that are either full time, part time, or flexible in nature. Growing businesses need all kinds of help, so knowing where to find the right person at a given time can make you an invaluable resource. This could also include knowing a network of freelancers, people who are retired or semiretired, stay-at-home parents, students, or individuals who are between jobs and looking for work. These are the same people who will get their hands dirty to make each of your investments more successful. They can also prove quite valuable to early-stage ventures that are looking to manage costs. If you have a SWAT team of specialized people at your disposal, you'll find yourself in great demand.

I met Thomas Quarre, a mobile user-interface and product designer, at a networking event a few years back. When he gave his pitch, I realized that I didn't know anyone else who designed mobile apps and our conversation stuck in my head. He also made sure to keep in touch, following up every couple of months, and always checking in to see how he could be of help to me. When a friend asked me if I knew anyone who specialized in interface design, I knew who to call. I couldn't yet comment on Thomas's work, so I suggested they meet to review his portfolio and see if there was chemistry. There was, so they worked together. A few months later, when I got a similar request, I recommended Thomas again, this time based on his contribution to my friend's company. Thomas has since collaborated with a number of people in my network. I appreciate that he never forgets to ask how he can help in return. He innately understands that working with me and the people in my network is a two-way street, so as an Angel, an Advisor, or just part of a network of like-minded people, I'm quick to recommend him. In doing so, I'm not just helping out a talented designer; I'm also adding value to the companies in my portfolio and deepening my relationships with my partners and the people on my team.

Enhance Your Credibility and Ace the Inevitable Google Test

Just as you'd never walk into a networking event wearing nothing but your underwear, you want to make sure that you are properly outfitted when it comes to the elements of networking that occur online. You can improve the probability of making impactful connections by enhancing your online credibility. At an absolute minimum, that means having an updated LinkedIn page that includes all of your credentials. Your LinkedIn profile will build upon the work you've done to craft a biography that is cohesive and that provides context for your experience and your ambitions. It's always wise, however, to let your past achievements speak for themselves. For some reason, people allow themselves to dive into a good deal of hyperbole on the Internet. Describing yourself as a "visionary entrepreneur" (that's a favorite) is fine if you are Bill Gates or Oprah, but it's a tad aggressive for the other 99.99 percent of the population. Instead, let your experience and your biography stand on their own merits. When you've framed them correctly, you'll be taken more seriously and the message will naturally come through.

If you plan to develop a strong brand as part of your 10%, you can take things a step further by carving out a corner of the Internet for yourself. People generally tend to take what they read online at face value, so that's a surprisingly effective way to bolster credibility in a given subject area. Your goal is simple: whenever someone Googles your name, you will emerge as an authority in your area of focus. That's the Google test. Whether you start a blog, write for industry-focused publications, tweet, speak at conferences, or even appear on television, all these activities build credibility, enhance your brand, and convince people that it's worth their time to meet you.

I was skeptical of this approach until I actually tried it. When I used to Google my name from time to time (admit it, you do, too), I would find all kinds of information about Patrick McGinnis, the former CEO of Nestlé Purina, but little about myself. After I resolved to make my name the most important brand on my business card, I also decided to upgrade my online presence.

My first step was a personal blog. I started writing about subjects that played to my strengths and then sent a few samples of my writing to the *Huffington Post*. It was a cold call, but they invited me to write for the platform. I also set up a Web site with my biography using a free online tool, and began writing for other online publications that were relevant to my interests. From that point forward, whenever I cold-called someone, I had the option of including a link to a relevant blog post or perhaps to my biography. I found that the response rate on e-mail requests climbed notably. If you Google me now, you find a pretty good series of links to various sources that, taken together, tell you a lot about me. It seems that Patrick McGinnis from Purina is no longer the only Patrick McGinnis in town.

Your desire to publicly declare your interest in a particular topic will depend on your comfort level with promoting your 10%. You may opt to keep your online presence independent from your 10%. You may also prefer to maintain a low profile online as a general rule. Regardless, there are a few basic steps you can take to enhance your credibility when you're presenting yourself to others. With a small investment of time and money, you can buy a domain name, set up a "corporate" e-mail, order business cards, and even crowdsource a logo. Most of those resources are free or inexpensive, but they will make a real difference. Given that these options are so user-friendly, I'm always a little surprised when someone hands me a flimsy-looking business card with a Hotmail address printed at the bottom. Why present yourself as an amateur when it's so cheap and easy to up your game?

Your Reputation Is Your Most Important Asset

Even if you've got a great set of business cards and a beautiful logo, your reputation trumps all. People will choose to work with you based on your track record and the quality of your references. Both of these considerations are essential to building a team and forging long-term partnerships. If nobody wants to work with you or your integrity is questionable, then you close doors and limit your options. Memories, like careers, are long, and our increasingly interconnected world is only getting smaller, so the decisions you make today will directly impact your ability to recruit high-quality talent to your efforts.

When Leslie Pierson launched a Kickstarter campaign for MEMI, a bracelet that vibrates when you get a phone call, the response from women with small children was tremendous. Leslie was a perfect face and Founder for the company. Not only was she a mom and a former management consultant, she was also an Angel investor and board member at 4moms, a tech company that makes next-generation baby products. Although she believed in her idea, she had to make a choice. With three small children under five, Leslie wanted to spend the vast majority of her time taking care of her family, so she recruited a full-time partner, Margaux Guerard, who had worked in senior marketing positions at Diane von Furstenberg and Bobbi Brown. With a partner like Margaux, Leslie was able to include MEMI in her 10% and devote the rest of her capacity to family obligations.

After preselling $100,000 worth of bracelets on Kickstarter, coverage in the *New York Times* and TechCrunch followed soon after. Yet despite all the buzz in the market, translating the concept into reality proved daunting. Even as they wrestled with the complexity of building computer hardware, the competition caught up, with products like the Apple Watch chipping away at a once uncontested market. Eventually, Leslie and Margaux made the difficult decision to cease operations and offer a refund to anyone who had preordered the item. They weren't required to do so, but they valued their reputations and wanted to do right by their customers.

Leslie acknowledges that MEMI was a learning experience, an adventure, and ultimately, a failure, but it's definitely not going to be her last business. Even though she had high hopes and very strong initial traction, she didn't let the early success go to her head. She ran the company lean, raised as little money as possible, and kept a cash reserve in case things didn't work out. As a result, she was able to uphold her moral obligation to her customers. Rather than taking a reputational hit, she's actually proven that when she does business, she stands by her partners and lives up to her responsibilities.

Every time you commit to a new venture, you're doing so with conviction. This isn't an exploratory mission or a hobby, it's a dimension of your life that deserves proper time and attention because it will become part of your personal track record. In fact, your level of commitment is of critical importance, since the successes in your 10% will open new doors in the rest of your life. Naturally, you'll face setbacks just like any other entrepreneur and you'll need to be resilient. When you face challenges or obstacles, it's your attitude that is going to pull you through and help you to keep going. As you'll see in the next chapter, if you're designing your 10% for the long run, you'll need to make sure that your head is in the game 100% of the time.

Chapter 9

Overcoming Obstacles

When you're a 10% Entrepreneur, you have a built-in backup plan in the form of your day job, but you're still an entrepreneur, in every sense of the word. You are putting yourself out there, taking risks, and pushing into uncharted territory. It is exhilarating, but it's never easy, especially when things don't go to plan or you meet resistance. That's why every entrepreneur, from 10% and up, finds that resilience and a firm commitment to a long-term vision are the most important tools of the trade.

Katy Tuncer knows all about resilience. While all her friends spent their gap years living out of a backpack, Katy polished boots and rushed out of bed for early-morning drills. Rather than taking a year off to "find herself," Katy found herself a coveted spot in a one-year program at the Royal Military Academy Sandhurst, the place where Princes William and Harry, Winston Churchill, and even King Hussein of Jordan got their starts. At the tender age of eighteen, Katy commanded a troop of soldiers, some of whom were more than twice her age.

A decade later, Katy once again yearned to apply her talents for the benefit of the public, so she took on a management role at the Metropolitan Police, popularly known as Scotland Yard. She also started a family, and as a lifelong athlete, she now appreciated how difficult it was for new mothers to focus on their own health, in addition to the well-being of their children. She wanted to find a way to empower busy women to find time for fitness, so she wrote a business plan for Ready Steady Mums, an online and real-world fitness program.

As she balanced the demands of her day job with caring for her children, Katy realized that if she was going to start her own company, she couldn't do it alone. She recruited technical talent, formed a board of Advisors, and rallied thousands of mothers who shared her vision. With her team and the community of moms on her side, Katy launched a crowdfunding campaign and raised nearly $100,000 from more than a hundred investors. The success of the campaign attracted the attention of the BBC, which in 2014 named her as one of its 100 Women.

Despite these promising beginnings, Ready Steady Mums was never able to reach sufficient scale to operate profitably, so Katy decided to shutter the company. Although she was disappointed, she was determined to wind down operations responsibly, so she contacted each of her largest investors personally to explain the situation. She was heartened by the depth of their support, especially when one of her larger investors told her to make sure to call him when she was next looking for capital. Katy also managed to sustain her mission by relaunching under the auspices of a nonprofit institution that monitors wellness for families across the United Kingdom. Although it was not viable as a for-profit business, Ready Steady Mums will still have a meaningful impact on new mothers across Britain.

Just as with full-time entrepreneurs, 10% Entrepreneurs can also fail. The difference is that 10% Entrepreneurs have far less to lose. When you put yourself on the line, invest your resources into a venture, and then stumble or face a roadblock, you're left with a decision: how will you react? When Katy realized that Ready Steady Mums was not a sustainable business, she faced the issue head-on, talked to her investors, and found a way to keep the mission alive for the sake of its loyal community and her vision. Ever the public servant, she wanted to achieve her objectives, so she remained focused on the big picture and made it happen. That's resilience.

Since your 10% represents just a portion of your professional life, when things don't go your way you can cut your losses and continue along your path. Still, even if you're not all in with respect to your time and your financial capital, you have made a significant emotional investment. This is the part of your career that most closely ties to your interests and the people that matter to you, so in that respect, you are most definitely all in. When it comes to the mental aspects of your work, the "10%" in 10% Entrepreneur doesn't matter, since everything you're doing counts for more. You're still an entrepreneur, so you'll need to be mentally tough, remain committed to your vision, and remember that each day of work, good or bad, takes you one step closer to your overall goals. You will have ups and downs, that's only natural, but when things don't go your way, you will take time to step back, remember why you're here in the first place, and keep your eyes on the prize.

Building resilience by working through obstacles will be an essential part of your strategy, as important as formulating your 10% Plan, conducting due diligence, and growing your network.

Sure, it's the touchy-feely part of the exercise, but it's also the part that more than any other comes down to you. For that reason alone, you must mentally prepare yourself for the psychological aspect of the game by knowing how to overcome impostor syndrome, avoid the paralysis of indecision, and bounce back when you face setbacks.

Avoid the Trap of Impostor Syndrome

Everybody knows the type of person who has a few business ideas that they have been carrying around and would love to pursue at some point. Very few people actually move beyond the discussion stage with any real sense of commitment. Instead, these ideas, and some of them are pretty good, get packed away and occasionally dragged out at cocktail parties. "You know what I'd really like to do one day?" the wantrepreneur will say with great enthusiasm. Then he will make you promise to tell no one before he launches into a detailed explanation of his proposed business model. A few minutes later, the conversation moves on and the business idea is packed away again until the next cocktail party. Then one day, when someone actually launches that very same business idea, the wantrepreneur will kick himself. If the idea is successful, he'll remind all his friends, "Remember when I told you about that idea? Now some lucky bugger is getting rich off MY idea!"

I was that guy. For the first decade of my career, I was firmly in the camp of people who preferred to leave work at the office. My day job was for making money. Evenings and weekends, while often punctuated by bouts of work, were my own. Why bother looking for more things to work on when I could use my free time to enjoy the fruits of my labor? It never even occurred to me that I could take pleasure from working on something on the side, or that my career could be larger than my day job. I never imagined that I could find that magic place where working on a real business opportunity wouldn't even *feel* like work.

Much of that mind-set stems from the fact that I'd never been exposed to the concept of pursuing personal business interests outside of the office. Both of my parents, in fact, everyone's parents I knew growing up, had a day job at one of the local companies or at the local branch of a large company. Work stopped the moment they left the office, the supermarket, the hair salon, the mall, the restaurant, or wherever they clocked their eight hours a day. Sure, some folks owned small businesses, but these were full-time businesses, like a small retail shop or the local Dairy Queen franchise. I'd been socialized to believe that you worked for a company or you ran a small business. Either way, you derived your livelihood from that endeavor and then allocated the rest of your time toward family, hobbies, and other pursuits.

If you've never really viewed yourself as an entrepreneur, changing your mind-set takes time, even if you've become successful in another field. One of the hardest things about exploring new ventures is the temptation to feel outgunned when you're meeting with people from well-known organizations. Sure, you've got experience and relationships, but it's easy to feel intimidated when you're putting *yourself* out there rather than representing a corporate brand on a business card. As a 10% Entrepreneur, you will constantly be pitching to people, telling them what you can bring to the table, seeking to establish credibility based on your past experiences, your relationships, and your vision. For many people, it's jarring to promote themselves after spending years selling a corporate brand and leveraging the kind of monolithic image that companies, especially large companies, project. Even your language will be different. Rather than starting sentences with "The firm" or "We," sentences will now start with "I."

When you're used to the comfort of your company's reputation, its nice offices, or its long and storied brand, operating in the absence of those things can make you a little insecure. In fact, it's completely natural to feel like you're an impostor when you're first starting out. I certainly did. Settling into your new-found autonomy takes some work. When you operate outside of your day job, there is greater uncertainty, but you step up to the plate and take what comes to you. You will wrestle with external factors and events beyond your control, but no matter what happens, the ultimate responsibility lies squarely on your shoulders.

Unless you have a highly evolved level of confidence, it's completely natural to wonder whether the person sitting across the table from you is going to take you seriously. When you're first getting started, you're selling an idea, after all. Whether you're an Angel, an Advisor, or a Founder, you're new to the game. Even if you're more than capable of everything you're setting out to achieve, you might worry that you're not "real" enough. It's stressful to feel like you have to "fake it 'til you make it."

Feeling like an impostor can actually be a healthy emotion, as long as you keep your doubts in check. It shows some humility, helps to keep you grounded, and motivates you to get going so that you can reach a place where you're strong and self-assured. It's also unnecessary. When you have a 10% Plan, you know where you're going and how to get there. By adding credible experience to the mix, most people will take you at face value. It helps if they know you from your day job, or some other facet of life, since they'll already be familiar with your capabilities.

Even if it's a first meeting, if you've got the guts to put yourself out there and you've got your story down, people will respect you for it. By agreeing to speak with you in the first place, they are clearly open-minded and willing to invest the time to find areas of mutual interest. From that point, it all comes down to having confidence and a solid pitch to ensure that you make the most of the opportunity. As I've said before, the image you project to the world is very much how others will see you. When you sit across the table in that very first meeting, you will quickly sense what you're putting out there based on the questions you're asked. Take note of these questions and adjust your approach, answering them in advance in future meetings. By eliminating areas of doubt, you will only enhance your presentation and your pitch.

You can also take some of the pressure off by remembering that your 10% is a work in progress. You will constantly be trying new things, testing ideas, going with what works well, and throwing out what doesn't. The minute I accepted the fact that my 10% was basically an early-stage venture and I was its Founder, I somehow felt freer. I had a 10% Plan, but I didn't have to know all the answers all the time. I could take risks, think outside the box, and ask for help, because that was what you're supposed to do when you're running a startup. I could also go back to the drawing board and make adjustments as I learned and improved. Armed with that realization, I felt more secure and better prepared to keep on and carry on when I encountered obstacles.

When You Feel Stuck, Trust in Your Plan

In June 2014, a message popped into my in-box from a name I didn't recognize. It was an e-mail from a journalist, Ben

Schreckinger, who was researching the history of the term FOMO, or Fear of Missing Out, for *Boston* magazine.[1] He tracked its origin to an article I wrote back in 2004, when I was a student. That was well before Facebook inflicted FOMO as the neurosis of choice for an ever-connected society. Social media didn't even really exist back then, but we still had plenty of fuel for our insecurities. My classmates and I had just lived through the dot-com crash and the 9/11 attacks. We were all a little traumatized, so we subconsciously resolved to live every minute to the max, whether we enjoyed ourselves or not.

The whole thing actually started with FOBO, or Fear of a Better Option. It was the term I came up with to explain the fact that everyone I knew at school was always looking for something better. Not just content with good, we wanted to trade up to great. You couldn't have a conversation with somebody without noticing that their eyes were scanning the room to figure out whom to talk to next. We were all about option value, usually just for the sake of having option value, and it was pretty insufferable. We didn't want to commit in case something better came along. FOMO was basically the opposite extreme. We were so afraid of missing out on some fun and unique experience that we'd say yes to everything. That's how you'd end up double or triple booking yourself on nights when you probably should have just stayed home.

FOMO and FOBO are irreconcilably opposing forces, the antithesis of yin and yang, and can drive a person toward a paralytic state I call FODA, or Fear of Doing Anything. They are the outcome of a mind-set that seeks optimization over action. FOMO and FOBO are especially dangerous when you're first starting to work on new ventures. Part of you wants to get something done, to make that first deal or investment, in order to break the ice and get started. Yet if you give in to FOMO, you risk committing to an opportunity for the wrong reasons. You should only say yes to a project because you believe in its fundamentals, not because you feel pressure to get involved lest you miss out. On the other hand, if you allow FOBO to creep into your strategy, you will waste valuable time waiting around for the perfect opportunity—an opportunity that doesn't actually exist. There's no such thing. That's why Goldilocks would make a lousy 10% Entrepreneur.

Although there is real value in keeping your options open at least for a period, choosing one opportunity or set of opportunities and closing down other potential pathways is essential. As a 10% Entrepreneur, you will continually weigh the relative risks and benefits associated with a variety of potential opportunities. Rarely is an opportunity so compelling that it can be considered a slam dunk. Even if you're Warren Buffett and have whole teams of people working for you, making investments still comes down to taking a leap of faith, since some of the factors at play are simply out of your hands. You can acknowledge all the gray areas, but you cannot let them paralyze you.

That's where your 10% Plan saves the day. Over the course of this book, you've invested your energy and your intellect to put together a 10% Plan that is tailored to your objectives, your resources, and your interests. Remember, when you are deciding whether to engage in a project, you're not making the decision on *relative* terms, but rather on *absolute* terms. As a result, you can avoid FOMO or FOBO entirely by trusting in the fact that your process permits you to evaluate each opportunity on a discrete basis. You will follow your plan, build your team, and put your process to work. Once you've done that, your homework—and your judgment—will drive your thinking and you will make your ultimate decision based on the merits: does this venture pass the test or not?

Consider the story of Peter Barlow. Peter had been burned twice by the time he started chatting with the founder of Silvercar on a flight. Rather than dismiss the idea as too risky or fall in love with the concept without doing his homework, he followed a plan. He checked on his potential partner's background, spent a lot of time on due diligence, and then recruited an experienced entrepreneur from the travel industry to come on board. So even though he was excited and ready to roll up his sleeves and get to work from the moment he saw the business plan, he always followed his 10% Plan, from assessing his resources to activating his investment process and his team.

What About Failure?

As you know, when you're an entrepreneur, you accept that failure is part of the process of building businesses. Even if you're wildly successful in the end, there will be plenty of moments when you'll feel like you're going to fail. Entrepreneurship is about experimentation, so finding out what *doesn't* work is often the only way to determine what *does* work. Sometimes, however, no amount of experimentation, hard work, and planning can make a venture successful. Like it or not, you're going to fail.

While failure does indeed "suck," when it's in your 10%, the impact on your overall career is limited. Still, you will need to take steps to limit any collateral damage by engaging with each of your partners to address any unresolved issues. As you saw with Katy Tuncer of Ready Steady Mums and with Leslie Pierson of MEMI, the way you behave when things go wrong can have a powerful impact on your reputation. Doing right by your partners and the other stakeholders in your business will say a lot about your character as a professional. You will also try to understand what went wrong so that you can avoid making similar mistakes elsewhere in your 10%. Finally, you'll seek to preserve the option to collaborate with the same set of people in the future, assuming that they were good partners. You'll all be wiser for your shared experience, so you can increase the odds of success the next time around.

As I wrote at the beginning of this book, I truly believe that 10% Entrepreneurs aren't born, they're made. Part of that process is failing and starting over again. Even when you face challenges, if you stay committed to your plan and to your vision, you will make steady progress. Over time, your resources will expand, your investment process will work more efficiently, and your network will become more powerful. You'll develop resilience, bouncing back from setbacks and operating with confidence. When all these factors come together, your machine will run faster and more smoothly, and you will see your investments pay off in ways you could never have imagined. In that sense, you'll have arrived. So what will be next? How will you sustain your momentum? In the last chapter, we will turn our attention to the core principles that will guide you over the long run.

Chapter 10

Winning the Long Game

N ow that you have your plan and you've marshaled your resources and your team, you're ready to accept the challenge and become a 10% Entrepreneur. This final chapter focuses on the values that will serve as guideposts in your future endeavors. Throughout this book, you've heard about mind-set, whether in terms of time, money, or the way that you build and manage your 10%. I've focused so much on mind-set because, in a fundamental sense, that's the new constraint to entrepreneurship. As little as a decade ago, there were plenty of other barriers to worry about if you wanted to start a new venture. You had to pay for prohibitively expensive technology and infrastructure. You were also limited by where you lived, since in many places you had fewer options when it came to finding talent and capital. Those obstacles no longer exist as they once did. The challenge today is to build something that is sustainable and that will create value, both financial and personal, over the course of your career.

Having grown up between Lebanon and the United States, Omar Chatah knows that entrepreneurs often flourish in the places where life is the most unpredictable. That's what makes Lebanon such a compelling market for entrepreneurship. When you have to rely on creativity and stamina just to navigate the mundane tasks of daily life, the challenges that come with launching a new venture don't seem that dramatic. Still, when Omar wanted to start something of his own, his father gave him some advice: If you want to pursue a sustainable path, save enough money to finance a business yourself.

Although that wasn't exactly what Omar wanted to hear, he opted for patience over passion, put his head down, and kept working at a software company in San Francisco. Then in December 2013, everything changed. His father, a politician, was assassinated in a car bombing in Beirut. In the aftermath of the attack, Omar found himself questioning the direction of his life. Impatience gnawed at him. He was still young, so what was holding him back from taking risks? You never know when something horrible is going to happen, so why wait?

He resolved to get serious about his business idea, a dating app called Hayati that adapts time-honored Arab dating practices to the smartphone world. Working at night and over weekends, Omar researched the process of starting a company, protecting intellectual property, and developing the associated software. After slashing his living expenses so that he could fund Hayati from his savings, he resigned from his day job. Six months later, when Omar visited Beirut, he discovered a changing city. The nascent local technology scene was taking off and he could hire high-quality software developers for far less than in the

United States. As he networked, he found himself interviewing for jobs. The timing made perfect sense. After building the app full time for the last six months, the most intense hours were now behind him and he could grow Hayati on the side.

Omar now manages an accelerator program that selects and mentors promising early-stage businesses and then sends them to London. At its heart, the program serves as a bridge for ideas, capital, and talent between Lebanon and the wider world. The country may be located in a tricky neighborhood, but it is an emerging regional hub for technology and innovation, and Omar operates at its center. His new role provides a sustainable platform that allows him to dedicate meaningful time to Hayati all while hedging his downside risk, earning a good living, and doing something important for his country.

The Guiding Principles of the 10% Entrepreneur

Omar's story brings together many of the themes explored in this book. All his decisions have been deliberate and he made and followed a plan. He's also structured his life and career in a way that plays to his strengths. As someone with one foot in Lebanon and another overseas, his roles at UK Lebanon Tech Hub and at Hayati leverage his unique set of talents when it comes to building bridges between the Arab world and the West. Moreover, his responsibilities at both places are completely symbiotic and he can build his startup without putting all his eggs in one basket. Like any good 10% Entrepreneur, his objectives are clear, his strategy is integrated, and his approach is deliberate. Looking at each of his decisions, you can tell that he's committed to winning the long game.

Once you finish this chapter and close this book, you have an option. You can put it back on the physical or digital bookshelf, or you can begin. That's where mind-set matters. It's what gets you from daydream to action. It takes you to the place where you are starting, doing, and making things happen. I hope you're convinced that it's time to get going. Look around you, learn from others, join their teams, then build your own 10%.

As you've seen over the course of this book, there is no one type of 10% Entrepreneur. They live all over the world, operate in a wide range of industries, and come from a variety of backgrounds. The one common thread is that all of these people look for opportunity and then make things happen. From that point forward, they take calculated risks, learn from their mistakes, and improve. With that in mind, this chapter will leave you with a set of guiding principles that represent the collective wisdom of the men and women who are on the front lines of the 10% movement. They are your compass and your map, and you can always return to this chapter to make sure that you stay on course.

Always Act with Integrity, Especially When It Comes to Your Employer

Your 10% provides you with myriad benefits, but it doesn't pay your salary. You cannot build your 10% at the expense of your full-time job. When conflicts arise, your day job must come first without question, since continued success there is the main reason you have the ability to work on outside projects. You have the financial capital and the stability to take risks. You also benefit from credibility, a base of contacts, and the skills that you will apply as you engage in entrepreneurial ventures. As long as you continue to nail it at your day job and play by the rules, your employer will value the insights that you bring back to the office. Before long, your colleagues may start to ask you if they can collaborate on some of your projects. All of that is possible if you give your best, both inside and outside the office.

Beware of gray areas. Gray areas lead to potential conflicts of interest. Your employer shouldn't pick up the bill for your personal business activities. You should never compete with your employer or take opportunities for yourself that rightfully belong in the province of your day job. Conduct business for your 10% over personal e-mail rather than your firm's e-mail, and avoid using corporate resources for your own purposes. The money you save on photocopies or office supplies could cost you dearly. If your firm requires you to disclose personal investments or business activities, be forthright. The minute your 10% breaches ethical or professional codes of conduct, either written or unwritten, you're out of bounds. It's game over. There is no room for error when it comes to professional ethics.

Finally, depending on your path, you may find that at some point it's difficult to balance the demands of your 10% and your day job. It's at this point that you've got to decide if you can continue to excel in all your activities. If you decide you want to pursue your 10% activities full time, you might be surprised that you can structure a soft landing with your employer. Firms struggle to find people they trust and they usually fight to hold on to their best employees. Much like Dipali Patwa of Masala Baby, you may find that your firm will allow you work on a flexible schedule while you focus more energy on a new venture.

Stick to Your Knitting

By playing to your strengths, you will focus on areas that you understand and enjoy, and that are integrated with the rest of your life. One of the clear benefits of that strategy is that you can have confidence that you're not going to stray too far from your areas of expertise. You'll stay focused and avoid the perils of FOMO and FOBO. Of course, there's nothing inherently wrong with wanting to pursue a project that is completely unrelated to your core skills. It's not inconceivable that you could dream up some big idea that has nothing to do with your present life, make a go of it, and become wildly successful. In the immortal words of Justin Bieber, "Never say never." It's just that it's rather hard to opt for that kind of strategy when you're working part time.

Choosing opportunities that are integrated with your life allows you to get up to speed quickly and make the right connections. In the parlance of venture capitalists, doing what you do best, or sticking to your knitting, greatly increases your chances of success. It will also make you far more efficient. The further you get from the industries you know and the people you trust, the more work you'll need to put into a venture. That's what makes having an integrated strategy so powerful. When you think about the types of activities that Hillyer Jennings, Luke Holden, Josh Newman, Dipali Patwa, Mildred Yuan, Diego Saez-Gil, and Katy Tuncer chose for their 10%, you realize how seamlessly those businesses fit into the rest of their lives.

If you do want to shift your focus to a new area and build additional skills, you can do so from a position of strength by drawing on the expertise you apply in your day job. Peter Barlow used his legal acumen to bridge his way into the business world.

His work at Silvercar was informed by his knowledge of corporate law, but he also brought a diversity of know-how to the table. Leslie Pierson leveraged her experience as a management consultant and a new mother to take a seat on the board of 4moms. This gave her critical early insights into patents and intellectual property that were invaluable in the early days of MEMI. When you're jumping across industries, you may need to take intermediate steps. It's not an instant gratification strategy, but it's a smart way to migrate your interests and network into an area where you've always wanted to build connectivity.

Look for Ways to Break Out of Your Comfort Zone

The flip side of sticking to your knitting is taking risks. Just because you're doing what you do best doesn't mean that you will always play it safe. Entrepreneurial ventures are inherently risky, so exploring your boundaries is part of the exercise. The difference is that you'll do so from a place of strength, by leveraging your resources, your investment process, and your network. There will be times when you'll be uncomfortable or uncertain, but thanks to the work you've done as you've read this book, you'll feel confident that you've got everything you need to operate in those circumstances.

When it comes to leaving your comfort zone, Alex Torrenegra takes the honors. When he moved from Colombia to the United States, he left behind a good life. He owned an IT company that had grown to twenty-five employees, lived in the best part of Bogotá, and even had his own car, a luxury that was unheard of among his friends. He left all those comforts behind to move to the United States and trade his CEO title for a bucket and a mop at McDonald's. He made this choice because he believed it would be the best way to eventually lead a groundbreaking technology business. It took him a little while, but he made it to Silicon Valley and he and Tania Zapata now own just that kind of company. It was a risk, but it's clearly paid off. You can take risks, too, but you don't have to move thousands of miles and upend your life to take chances. You can start much smaller and still see tremendous benefits.

Launching a new venture as part of your 10% doesn't just allow you to segregate the risk of failure from the rest of your career. It also provides you with a place to experiment, fail, pivot, and relaunch. Entrepreneurs who snatch success from the jaws of failure often credit a well-timed pivot, basically a change in their business model, for creating the conditions for their ultimate success. The steep decline in the cost of starting businesses in many industries also makes it possible for you to try, try again. You can test ideas, build prototypes, and even launch a product on a small budget. If your thesis doesn't prove out or your product doesn't take off, all is not lost. Even if you fail, your failure will be self-contained, which will limit the fallout and its effects on the rest of your career. Your 90% remains intact and provides the stability and credibility for you to step away, regroup, and come back another day.

Take Charge of Your Education

For my first few years working in finance, I was embarrassed to admit that I didn't really understand accounting. If accounting was indeed the "language of business," I was far from fluent. That's not an ideal situation if you want to actually get somewhere on

Wall Street. Even though I could plug all the numbers into a template and get to the right answer, I was faking it. Everyone else seemed to know what they were doing, but I was afraid to ask for help. What if someone figured out that I was an impostor? Finally, after four years of scratching my head, I bought an accounting book and read it from front to back. In doing so, I finally saw how all the pieces fit together, and I realized that I wasn't naturally bad at accounting. I just never had the chance to learn it properly until I took matters into my own hands.

When you leave your comfort zone, you will encounter new concepts and unfamiliar jargon. While you will develop the kind of street smarts that can only come with learning in the real world, you will also be in charge of your own education. Every time you look at a new opportunity, you will need to dig in and learn new things, but you will also run into recurring issues, such as legal and financial matters. The good news is that there are many good books, blogs, and Web sites that will help you learn and gain confidence in these fields. Some of my favorite resources are included in the notes section at the end of this book. You can also find help in the real world by joining an angel group or partnering with people whose skills are complementary to yours. Finally, you can take classes at a local college or enroll in specialized online courses covering nearly any topic you can imagine.

It's never too early to start building your 10%, and working on part-time entrepreneurial ventures can be highly complementary to a student lifestyle. When you're a student, you are immersed in an environment where lots of other people are laser focused on personal and professional growth. You also have considerable educational materials and research tools at your disposal and you can draw on the expertise and energy of fellow students and professors to gather knowledge and resources. You may also have greater flexibility in your schedule than when you're working full time. In this way, Hillyer Jennings used his free time at law school to develop the business plan and the prototype for Wrist Tunes. Similarly, one of Diego Saez-Gil's partners at Bluesmart, Brian Chen, joined the company just before entering an MBA program at the Massachusetts Institute of Technology. Once classes started, he worked on Bluesmart and his degree concurrently, leveraging the resources of the MIT community for the benefit of the business. Then, after Bluesmart really took off, he put his studies on hold to join the company full time.

Spread the Wealth

When you embrace an entrepreneurial mind-set, you see opportunity in places where you never saw it before. You also quickly learn that this is not a zero-sum game. Your power comes from your expertise, but it also comes from your network. You will do your homework and trust your intuition, but you will actively draw on the talents, ideas, networks, and goodwill of others to make this happen. That's how to make your 10% scalable. You cannot be in all places at all times. You cannot know all the facts. That's why you have a team. You are designing a self-sustaining machine that will run on the energy and brains of the people you recruit to work with you. These individuals will take roles throughout your 10%. They will invest with you, advise you, source for you, and even work on projects for you or the companies in your portfolio. Gavin Newton-Tanzer, the after-school education entrepreneur in China, recognized early on that the value of his company would grow immeasurably if he surrounded himself with the right people. He didn't rest until he conveyed his vision to them and brought them on board.

There's no reason to keep all the benefits of your hard work, and the contributions of all the people on your team, for yourself. By continuing to look for ways to bring new talent into your 10%, you're expanding the pie for everyone on your team— including yourself. You're also giving yourself access to people whose networks, skills, and interests are complementary to your own. In exchange, you will offer them opportunities to take part in your portfolio of activities for the benefit of their wallets and their resumés. You're not in the business of making money just for yourself; you want everyone you know to come out a winner. You're not a wildebeest and you don't follow the crowd, but you're willing to run in a herd if the people around you share your values and watch your back. When you do find those people, explore avenues to partner with them, offer them opportunities to become Angels or Advisors, and try to align everyone's incentives by working together on the best projects you can find. If you are generous and find ways to share upside with the people who work with you, they will likely return the favor.

Surround Yourself with People Who Bring Out the Best in You

Your 10% is the most personal aspect of your career. That means that it's a place where you can choose your partners. Businesses are about ideas and they are about people. They fail under the weight of inadequate human capital, misaligned incentives, and personal conflicts. If you're considering working with a new partner, you will want to do your due diligence, put everything on the table, and join forces with someone who shares your values. If you face financial constraints or have trouble finding the right people, look to those you trust to fill the void. For example, you can collaborate with friends, family, former colleagues, and other people who are important to you. They have your best interests in mind and they're far more willing to give you the benefit of the doubt than somebody who doesn't know you. They are also more likely to be completely honest with you when you're off the right track. In addition, since you'll be operating in your 10%, the stakes are far lower than if you were collaborating on a full-time endeavor. This allows you to figure out if you work well together before you make a deeper commitment.

It's no surprise that a number of the companies profiled in this book were started by entrepreneurs who worked closely with the people in their lives. Luke Holden split the initial investment to open his first store with his father. His younger brothers, Bryan and Michael, now work at the company. Bryan, who is a partner in the business and oversees the build-outs of the Luke's Lobster stores, is even drawing on that experience to design and make custom furniture as part of his 10%. Plus, it seems like half the town of Cape Elizabeth, Maine, works at Luke's Lobster at this point. Similarly, Hillyer Jennings's brothers down in Georgia help him with the warehousing and fulfillment for Wrist Tunes.

Your 10% should make your life richer and more interesting, but not at the expense of your relationships. Even if you don't put your friends and family to work and recruit them to your ventures, you still need their support. Building your 10% will require some sacrifice. No matter how much you enjoy every moment of your work, your significant other or your children may not. You will have more going on in your life and you will dedicate time and energy to your business. If you can find ways to involve your loved ones in your 10%, you can make that time count for more. Alex and Tania partnered to build Bunny Inc., and they spend far more time together than they would if they were working on separate entrepreneurial ventures. Similarly, Josh Newman and his wife, Lisa, decided to create a digital agency as a way to have fun together while building a real business.

Follow the Golden Rule

Entrepreneurship is as much an endurance sport as anything else. When you're starting a new venture, raising capital, and trying to land initial customers, you're going to grow accustomed to hearing the word "no." You'll also get used to dealing with people who ignore you, forget you, or are generally hard to pin down. People are busy, and if you're not included on their list of priorities, they will just disappear. If you're an Angel, you'll find yourself on the other side of this equation. You will meet with companies, some of which will come with half-baked ideas, poorly conceived business plans, or mediocre management teams. At a time when just about anyone can put together a PowerPoint deck, a surprisingly small percentage of the opportunities that enter your in-box will be truly interesting. That's why you should waste as little time as possible on screening. If you don't screen aggressively, you can invest hours learning about business opportunities that have little chance of meeting your criteria.

Rejection is an eye-opening experience. When I was working for large firms, I always felt a bit bad when I said no to someone, but I didn't really *know* what it felt like to have somebody say no to my idea. When I sat on the other side of the table and tried to sell YouTube partnerships at Real Influence, I got a taste of what I was missing. It was educational.

There's nothing wrong with saying no, but there is no reason to be rude, disrespectful, or unresponsive. You are playing the long game. You are planting seeds that may only prove fruitful many years down the line. The person with the poorly conceived business plan today may be the CEO of a very attractive company one day soon. Your consideration, or lack thereof, will be remembered. If you want to continue to get invited to the party, behave yourself.

Following the Golden Rule also extends to following through on your commitments. Talk is cheap. If you promise to make an introduction, wire funds, or reserve a certain number of hours per month as an Advisor, you need to show up. If you're not present and engaged, what's the point of building your 10%? This is the part of your career in which you can make choices, follow your interests, and build something for yourself. If your 10% feels like an obligation rather than a privilege, then it's time to rethink your strategy.

Make Your 10% an Ongoing and Dynamic Part of Your Life

When it comes to 10% Entrepreneurs, Stephen Siegel is a legend. He's a self-made real estate mogul who rose to the role of chairman of global brokerage at CBRE, the world's largest commercial real estate services company. As a self-described "deal junkie," he's been building his 10% since before I was in diapers. Stephen made his first investment when he was in his twenties, joining two senior partners with deeper pockets to acquire a hotel in midtown Manhattan. Now, four decades later, he is currently invested in more than one hundred projects, from real estate to restaurants and beyond.

If you think in terms of decades and not months or years, your 10% can come to represent a meaningful part of your professional and personal life. Before I met Stephen, I'd heard of him, since his 10% is part of his public persona. He is one of the partners behind the revival of the saloon P. J. Clarke's, a New York institution, in partnership with the actor Timothy Hutton and late New York Yankees' owner George Steinbrenner. He even owns part of a minor-league baseball team. When one of his former clients decided to buy the team, Stephen joined the investor group. A longtime lover of baseball, he knew he'd probably never be in the position to be part owner of a major-league team. This was the next best thing, and he now has five championships under his belt.

In the old days, you had to retire to pursue your dreams. Now, it's quite the opposite. The age range of 10% Entrepreneurs profiled in this book spans nearly fifty years. You're never too young to start and you never have to retire. If you love what you're doing, you can keep going, tailoring all your side activities to your passions and your strengths, whether you've got a day job or not. By continuing to invest, as Stephen has done throughout his career, your 10% will become part of your identity. It reflects who you are as a person and a professional and it's the only part of your career that you will take with you no matter where you go.

Forget About Convincing the Critics

Back when my father was growing up in my hometown in Maine, there was a man who was known around town by the name of

Jellerson. He was a well-known character because he ambled up and down the country roads collecting empty bottles that he would cash in for money. Every so often, he would walk nearly twenty miles to visit friends in the next town over. If a car stopped along the route to ask him if he needed a ride, he would tip his hat and turn them down. "Thanks," he'd say, "but I'm in a hurry." With that answer, everyone around town thought he was an eccentric at best and a lunatic at worst.

The first time I heard my dad tell that suburban legend, I couldn't help but laugh and shake my head. Growing up in small-town New England has me accustomed to offbeat characters. That comes with the territory. The more I thought about Jellerson, however, the more I wondered if he was onto something. When you're an entrepreneur, you must decide where you're going and then plan how to get there. You're not going to take the same path as everyone else. Although you won't follow the traditional route and other people may not quite get what you're doing, you're moving forward, full steam, in your own way. Maybe walking is just fine if you're in a hurry.

When you're doing something new or unconventional, a surprising number of critics come out of the woodwork. They may wonder why you need to spend your free time working. If you're working and they're not, what does that say about them? You may also find that your new venture elicits strange reactions from your friends and colleagues. Everybody's got an opinion, and they'll be happy to tell you why your idea will never work or your new product is flawed. I was shocked at the number of friends who contacted me just to tell me everything that was wrong with the Bluesmart suitcase when the company first launched its crowdfunding campaign. It was too big, too small, too heavy, too light, too complicated, or too simple. After achieving more than $2 million in presales on Indiegogo, some of those very same people then complained that I never invited them to invest!

Don't waste your time trying to convince people who don't believe in what you're doing. If you've got the support of the important people in your life, specifically the people who will be affected by your choices, that's all you need. Everyone else may take a little time to catch up, but that's not your problem. It's always helpful to have feedback, ideas, and constructive criticism. You might even learn something that enables you to avoid problems. Or you may not learn anything. Rather than burning calories trying to convince people that what you're doing is worth the time and the effort, put that energy into your 10%. Once things are up and running, you won't have to convince anyone. They'll be calling and asking you how to get involved and join your team.

You Have Only One Life: Have Fun and Make It Interesting

Entrepreneurship takes you to unexpected places. You meet fascinating people whom you'd never otherwise encounter. You become an expert in things you'd never have expected to know much about. You gain confidence in your skills. You allow yourself to be interesting. If you've spent years taking the same commute, following the same schedule, and wearing the same suit, you'll enjoy a little variety in your life. Building new things, meeting new people, and surprising yourself never gets old, so embrace the chance to do something out of the ordinary.

One of the side benefits of entrepreneurship is the "cocktail party effect." When you're working on a project that gets you excited, that energy is contagious. If you're willing to share your stories, you will find that you're soon at the center of the conversation. That's how I met Peter Barlow. We were at opposite ends of a holiday party talking about our 10% pursuits, when someone approached me, gestured to Peter, and spoke those words that are now music to my ears: "You should meet Peter . . . he's exactly the kind of person you're writing about."

William Langer, a lawyer in Washington, D.C., once told me that a headhunter instructed him to remove all of his "interests" from his resumé. She was concerned that potential employers would think he was too "interesting." Perhaps they would pass him over out of concern that he wouldn't devote all his energies to the firm. I think the opposite is true. Being interesting isn't just a side benefit of 10% Entrepreneurship, it's also a strategy. Your interests can be a vital part of the story when you're working on your 10%, since you ideally want to leave an impression with everyone you meet. If you're memorable, the next time someone finds a compelling opportunity that could fit your criteria, they'll think of you and drop you a line. That conversation may just be the spark that results in the next opportunity, the next collaboration, and the next great adventure. For some people that kind of thing happens every once in a while, but not for you. For you, it will become routine. That's just another day in the life of a 10% Entrepreneur.

Acknowledgments

If you ever want to develop a keener sense of gratitude, try writing a book. It should be the loneliest of endeavors, and at times it is, but mostly you are sustained by the kindness and encouragement of others.

The 10% Entrepreneur is the result of several years of discussions and experiments. First and foremost, I must thank everyone in my 10%, all the 10% Entrepreneurs in this book, as well as the many individuals who provided background interviews. All of your contributions and ideas were instrumental to me.

Jason Haim, it's hard to imagine having a friend with stronger intellect or a better compass—never better.

Geoff Gougion, having the Digital Don Draper in my corner is such a privilege.

Marcelo Camberos, you taught me so much about entrepreneurship, 10% or otherwise. *Sos un maestro—El Gato.*

Acknowledgments

Samara O'Shea, you were my writing Sherpa and the first person to tell me I just might have a book in me.

Xin Zeng and Ben Schreckinger, you were the catalysts; Danielle Hootnick Kaufman and Katherine Liu, our many conversations were so critical to shaping my thinking; and Irene Hong Edwards, you've kept me sane and social for over a decade.

Fraser Simpson, you reminded me that to play the Great Game, you've got to be fearless.

Chellie Pingree, from one Mainer to another, I can't thank you enough. Also, a big thank-you to Will Blodgett and Carolyn Tisch Blodgett, for arranging a very chilly and productive period of writing.

Susan Segal, working together was an unforgettable adventure to which I owe so much of the content of this book.

Luciana Isella, that amazing gift, handed to me on a street in Buenos Aires, brought me lots of good luck and maybe even a little divine intervention.

For reasons big, small, and medium, I must also thank Greg Prata, Felix Dashevsky, John Leone, Ben Wigoder, Michele Levy, Florencia Jimenez-Marcos, Terry Chang, Helen Coster, Jordon Nardino, Davalois Fearon, Allison Stewart, Lars Kroijer, Dan Mathis, Brad Saft, Amy Calhoun Robb, Jay Sammons, Ariel Arrieta, Gonzalo Costa, Andrew Watson, Fiona Aboud, Richard Baran, Debora Spar, Zia Chishti, Mohammed Khaishgi, Hasnain Aslam, Ben Wu, Nihar Sait, Sana Rezwan Sait, Santiago Tenorio, Chris Carey, and Ali Rashid, as well as Tom Clark, Phil Tseng, Suken Shah, and the entire Wobbly H family.

A special thanks also goes out to Luke Masuda, Nicolas Walters, Gary Crotaz, Vanessa Beckett, Josh Weedman, Andy Lee, Matthew Stoller, Cate Ambrose, and Leslie Pierson, for making introductions that helped me immeasurably.

To my godchildren, Finley Clark and Thomas Gougion: get ready to start your 10% in a few years.

Writing a book is a marathon, and with the team at Portfolio, I have the best coaches I could ever imagine. Adrian Zackheim, your support and vision have been a constant, and I'm grateful for both. Joel Rickett, you understood this idea instinctively and you, along with Niki Papadopoulos across the pond, took a chance on me. Emily Angell and Kary Perez, your early guidance made the book better from top to bottom. Will Weisser, Tara Gilbride, and Taylor Fleming, your creativity and energy have been invaluable. Last, but certainly not least, Bria Sandford, you came at just the right time and it made all the difference. It's great to have someone so, dare I say, flinty on Team 10%.

I must also thank my multitalented agent, Mildred Yuan, who understood and shaped this idea from day one. Every interaction is a pleasure and an education that brings out my best.

Finally, to my family: Mike McGinnis, I'm happy to have a brother whose advice always rings true. Robert and Sonia McGinnis, you were so insistent that I try writing that I gave in to your wishes, wrote half of a terrible novel, threw it away, and then started writing this book. For that and for so much more, thanks, Mom and Dad!

Glossary

10% Entrepreneur: A person who has a full-time job, but dedicates at least 10% of his time, and, if possible, capital, to investing, advising, and getting involved with entrepreneurial ventures on a part-time basis. This allows the person to create downside protection and upside opportunity. It also gives the person the opportunity to try new things, make life more fun, and develop an entrepreneurial skill set.

110% Entrepreneur: A full-time entrepreneur who also acts as a 10% Entrepreneur at the same time.

Advisor: A person who provides expertise, in the form of advice, connections, or specific skills, to entrepreneurial ventures in exchange for remuneration in the form of equity.

Aficionado: A 10% Entrepreneur who integrates entrepreneurship into his life in order to pursue a passion or an interest. While this individual does not choose to practice that passion full time, he wants to be able to explore it meaningfully and on par with others who are committed full time.

Glossary

Anchor tenant: The project or opportunity that gets you started as a 10% Entrepreneur. This endeavor will play to your strengths and represent something that you view as achievable within the scope of your resources.

Angel: A person who invests capital into entrepreneurial ventures in exchange for equity.

Due diligence: A comprehensive analysis and assessment of a business venture to determine its worthiness for investment.

Entrepreneurship, Inc.: The various forces that glamorize the process of starting and leading companies without realistically portraying the risks, costs, and challenges of such endeavors.

Equity: Ownership in a company by holding shares, or stock, of that company. Equity can appreciate over the long term to create value and wealth for the holder.

FOBO: Fear of a Better Option. The inability to commit to one activity, but instead keep all of your options open. It is a side effect of attempts at optimization.

FODA: Fear of Doing Anything. The combined effect of FOBO and FOMO, which leads to decision paralysis and despair.

FOMO: Fear of Missing Out. The inability to focus on one activity or endeavor out of a concern that something better is happening at the same time. It is a side effect of attempts at optimization.

Founder: A 10% Entrepreneur who starts and manages his own company.

Intellectual capital: The base of knowledge and skills that you bring to bear in your work as a 10% Entrepreneur.

Opportunity cost: The "cost" of a foregone opportunity in terms of forfeited benefits.

Sweat equity: Equity that is earned in exchange for time and expertise rather than financial capital.

Appendix

I hope that by reading this book you are taking the first steps in what will become a lifelong commitment to 10% Entrepreneurship. Please keep in touch and send me ideas, feedback, edits, comments, or questions. In order to continue the conversation, stay on top of updated information, and access resources that will help you in your work, find me online at:

Web site: www.patrickmcginnis.com
Twitter: @pjmcginnis—tag your tweet with #10percent
Facebook: www.facebook.com/The10PercentEntrepreneur

Appendix

Managing Financial Capital: Sample Spreadsheet Templates

CALCULATING FINANCIAL CAPITAL	CURRENT	YEAR 5
Cash and Liquid Investments		
Checking, Savings, CDs, Etc.		
Brokerage Accounts, Stocks, Etc.		
Other		
Total		
Long-term Investments		
Company Stock Plan, 401k, IRA, Etc.		
Real Estate		
10% Investments		
Other		
Total		
Total Financial Capital		
Expected Increases/Decreases (Net of Taxes)		
(+/-) Savings or Deficit (From Personal Budget)		
(+) Bonus		
(+) Sales of Assets (House, Car, Etc.)		
(+) Gift or Inheritance		
(-) Major Purchases		
(-) Down Payments (House, Car, Etc.)		
(+/-) Other		
Total		
Adjusted Total Financial Capital		

PERSONAL BUDGET	MONTHLY BUDGET	ANNUAL BUDGET
Income		
Salary		
Income from 10%		
Other Income		
Total Income		
Expenses		
Household: Mortgage/Rent, Insurance, Utilities		
Communications: Phone, Internet, TV		
Transportation: Car, Public Transport		
Personal/Family: Food, Clothing, Personal Items		
Education: Tuition, School Expenses		
Medical: Insurance, Other		
Leisure: Entertainment, Hobbies, Vacation		
Financial: Credit Card Payments, Student Loans, Other		
Other		
Total Expenses		
Savings or Deficit		

Sample Professional Biography

Patrick McGinnis is the managing partner of Dirigo Advisors, which provides strategic advice to investors and businesses operating in Latin America and other emerging markets. In this capacity, he has advised the World Bank and the International Finance Corporation on projects related to private equity and venture capital. In 2013, Patrick coauthored a World Bank Policy Working Paper titled "Private Equity and Venture Capital in SMEs in Developing Countries: The Role for Technical Assistance." He also serves on the Boards of Directors of The Resource Group and Socialatom Ventures, a seed investment fund based in Medellín, Colombia.

Additionally, Patrick is a 10% Entrepreneur, having made angel investments in companies in the United States and Latin America. These include: ipsy, Bluesmart, SATMAP, NXTP Labs, WeHostels, Everbright Media, the Fan Machine, Preference Labs, and Morton & Bedford. He also serves as an advisor to Bunny Inc., Bluesmart, Posto, Preference Labs, and Everbright Media.

Prior to founding Dirigo Advisors, he was a vice president of PineBridge Investments (formerly AIG Capital Partners), a global emerging-markets investment firm. At PineBridge, Patrick sourced, structured, executed, and monitored growth equity investments in Latin America, Central Europe, the Middle East, and Asia. Patrick also advised portfolio companies on matters including strategic and financial planning, capital structure, acquisitions, business development, and exit opportunities.

Before joining PineBridge, Patrick was an investment professional at JPMorgan Partners, working on the Latin America team in both New York and São Paulo. He served on the Board of Directors of Hispanic Teleservices Corporation, a Mexican outsourced contact center, and was an alternate director at Freddo S.A., Argentina's leading artisanal ice cream retailer. Patrick started his career as an investment banker in the Latin America group of Chase Manhattan.

An avid traveler, writer, and speaker, Patrick has visited more than seventy countries. He writes about travel, technology, and business for Forbes.com, the *Huffington Post, Boston* magazine, *Business Insider,* and the Latin America Venture Capital Association. He is a frequent speaker on the topics of entrepreneurship, venture capital, private equity, and emerging-markets investing, with appearances in the United States, Mexico, Colombia, Argentina, and Mozambique.

Patrick sits on the Board of Trustees of the New York Youth Symphony. He is a member of the Business Advisory Network of NESsT, a not-for-profit that develops sustainable social enterprises that solve critical social problems in emerging-market economies. He is also a Young Trustee of Atlas Corps, and sits on the Steering Committee of the Young Professionals of the Americas.

Patrick graduated magna cum laude from the School of Foreign Service at Georgetown University, where he served a one-year appointment as a Rotary Ambassadorial Scholar at the Universidad Torcuato di Tella in Buenos Aires, Argentina. He holds an MBA from Harvard Business School.

He is fluent in Spanish, Portuguese, and French.

Notes

Introduction

1 "UPDATE 1-AIG Chief: 'I Need All the Help I Can Get,'" Reuters, 18 Mar. 2009, www.reuters.com/article/2009/03/19/financial-aig-scene-idUSN 1832099720090319, accessed 16 Sept. 2015.

Chapter 1. One Job Is Not Enough

1 "Number of Jobs Held, Labor Market Activity, and Earnings Growth Among the Youngest Baby Boomers: Results from a Longitudinal Survey," Bureau of Labor Statistics, U.S. Department of Labor, 15 Mar. 2015, www.bls .gov/news.release/pdf/nlsoy.pdf, accessed 16 Sept. 2015.

2 Jeanne Meister, "Job Hopping Is the 'New Normal' for Millennials," *Forbes*, 14 Aug. 2012, www.forbes.com/sites/jeannemeister/2012/08/14/job -hopping-is-the-new-normal-for-millennials-three-ways-to-prevent-a-human -resource-nightmare/, accessed 16 Sept. 2015.

3 Justin Baer and Daniel Huang, "Wall Street Staffing Falls Again," *Wall Street Journal*, 19 Feb. 2015, www.wsj.com/articles/wall-street-staffing -falls-for-fourth-consecutive-year-1424366858, accessed 16 Sept. 2015.

4 Elizabeth Olson, "Burdened with Debt, Law School Graduates Struggle in Job Market," *New York Times*, 26 Apr. 2015, www.nytimes.com/2015/04/27 /business/dealbook/burdened-with-debt-law-school-graduates-struggle-in-job -market.html?smid=nytcore-iphone-share&smprod=nytcore-iphone.

5 Richard Gunderman and Mark Mutz, "The Collapse of Big Law: A Cautionary Tale for Big Med," *The Atlantic*, 11 Feb. 2014, www.theatlantic .com/business/archive/2014/02/the-collapse-of-big-law-a-cautionary-tale-for -big-med/283736/, accessed 16 Sept. 2015.
6 Susan Adams, "Why Do So Many Doctors Regret Their Job Choice?," *Forbes*, 27 April 2012, http://www.forbes.com/sites/susanadams/2012/04/27 /why-do-so-many-doctors-regret-their-job-choice/, accessed 20 Oct. 2015.
7 Dan Heath and Chip Heath have thoroughly explored corporate mythology in their excellent book *The Myth of the Garage*.
8 Brandon Lisy, "Steve Wozniak on Apple, the Computer Revolution, and Working with Steve Jobs," *Bloomberg BusinessWeek*, 4 Dec. 2014, www .businessweek.com/articles/2014-12-04/apple-steve-wozniak-on-the-early -years-with-steve-jobs, accessed 15 June 2015.
9 "73% of Startup Founders Make $50,000 Per Year or Less," *Compass*, 14 Jan. 2014, blog.startupcompass.co/73-percent-of-startup-founders-make -50-dollars-000-per-year-or-less, accessed on 16 Sept. 2015.
10 David Teten, "VC Perspective: How Long Before Angel Investors (and VCs) Exit?," pehub.com, 16 June 2015, www.pehub.com/2015/06/vc-perspective -how-long-before-angel-investors-and-vcs-exit/, accessed 16 Sept. 2015.
11 "It's Definitely a Marathon—Venture-Backed Tech IPOs Take Seven Years from First Financing," *CB Insights Blog*, 7 Nov. 2013, www.cbinsights.com /blog/venture-capital-exit-timeframe-tech/, accessed on 16 Sept. 2015.
12 Amar Bhide, "How Entrepreneurs Craft Strategies That Work," *Harvard Business Review*, 1 Mar. 1994, hbr.org/1994/03/how-entrepreneurs-craft -strategies-that-work, accessed on 16 Sept. 2015.
13 Ghosh looked at outcomes of companies that managed to raise at least $1 million in venture capital between 2004 and 2010.
14 Carmen Nobel, "Why Companies Fail—and How Their Founders Can Bounce Back," HBS Working Knowledge, 7 Mar. 2011, hbswk.hbs.edu/ item/6591.html, accessed on 23 Oct. 2015.
15 Bill Snyder, "Marc Andreessen," Stanford Graduate School of Business, *Insights*, 23 June 2014, www.gsb.stanford.edu/insights/marc-andreessen -we-are-biased-toward-people-who-never-give, accessed 1 Sept. 2015.

Chapter 2. All the Benefits Without the Pitfalls

1 "Start Me Up," *The Economist*, 7 July 2014, http://www.economist.com/ blogs/graphicdetail/2014/07/daily-chart-6, accessed on 25 Oct. 2015.
2 Formerly Elance-oDesk.

Chapter 3. The Five Types of 10% Entrepreneurs

1 Jeffrey Sohl, "The Angel Investor Market in 2014: A Market Correction in Deal Size," Center for Venture Research, 14 May 2015.

2 Joel Koetsier, "The Rise of the Angel Investor (Infographic)," VentureBeat, 19 Feb. 2013, venturebeat.com/2013/02/19/the-rise-of-the-Angel-investor -infographic/, accessed 16 Sept. 2015.

3 Nick Bilton and Evelyn M. Rusli, "From Founders to Decorators, Facebook Riches," *New York Times*, 1 Feb. 2012, www.nytimes.com/2012/02/02 /technology/for-founders-to-decorators-facebook-riches.html, accessed on 16 Sept. 2015.

Chapter 4. What Kind of 10% Entrepreneur Are You?

1 "FAQs for Angels & Entrepreneurs," Angel Capital Association, www.angel capitalassociation.org/press-center/Angel-group-faq/, accessed 16 Sept. 2015.

Chapter 5. Making the Most of Time and Money

1 David Mielach, "Americans Spend 23 Hours Per Week Online, Texting," Yahoo! News, 3 July 2013, news.yahoo.com/americans-spend-23-hours-per -week-online-texting-092010569.html, accessed 16 Sept. 2015.

2 Mary Meeker, "Internet Trends 2014—Code Conference," Kleiner Perkins Caufield & Byers, kpcb.com, 28 Mar. 2014, kpcbweb2.s3.amazonaws.com /files/85/Internet_Trends_2014_vFINAL_-_05_28_14-_PDF.pdf?1401286773, accessed 16 Sept. 2015.

3 Marianne Hudson, "Important Things to Know About Angel Investors—2014," Angel Capital Association, www.angelcapitalassociation.org/data/Documents /Resources/ACA-AngelBackground2014.pdf, accessed 16 Sept. 2015.

4 "How to Save Like the Rich and the Upper Middle Class (Hint: It's Not with Your House)," wsj.com, *Real Time Economics*, 26 Dec. 2014, www.wsj .com/articles/BL-REB-29827, accessed 16 Sept. 2015.

5 Katherine Muniz, The Motley Fool, "20 Ways Americans Are Blowing Their Money," *USA Today*, 24 Mar. 2014, www.usatoday.com/story/money /personalfinance/2014/03/24/20-ways-we-blow-our-money/6826633/, ac- cessed 16 Sept. 2015.

6 Douglas McIntyre, "Ten Things Americans Waste the Most Money On" 24/ 7WallSt.com, 24 Feb. 2011, 247wallst.com/Investing/2011/02/24/ten -things-americans-waste-the-most-money-on/, accessed 16 Sept. 2015.

7 It is entirely possible, for example, to invest a share of your retirement sav- ings, such as a 401k or an IRA, in your 10%.

8 David Teten, "How and Why to Be an Angel Investor," teten.com, teten .com/blog/2014/09/16/dave-kerpen-interview-how-and-why-to-be-an-angel -investor/.

9 John Waggoner, "Cash Is King for Long-term Investors?," *USA Today*, 30 July 2013, www.usatoday.com/story/money/personalfinance/2013/07/30/ cash-best-long-term-investment/2600495/, accessed 16 Sept. 2015.

Chapter 6. Playing to Your Strengths

1   Many thanks to Tony Deifell for introducing me to this poem.
2   I am grateful to Prof. Jan Rivkin of Harvard Business School for developing and teaching this essential course.
3   Devin Banerjee, "Wall Street's Gilded Maternity Perk: Nannies Fly Free," Bloomberg.com, 13 Aug. 2015, www.bloomberg.com/news/articles /2015-08-13/wall-street-s-gilded-maternity-perk-flying-nannies, accessed 16 Sept. 2015.

Chapter 7. Finding, Analyzing, and Committing to Ventures

1   Noam Wasserman's excellent book, *The Founder's Dilemmas: Anticipating and Avoiding the Pitfalls That Can Sink a Startup*, provides advice on how founders should structure their involvement in new ventures.
2   *The Entrepreneur's Guide to Business Law*, by Constance Bagley, is an indispensable resource on these topics, covering everything you will need with respect to legal topics as a 10% Entrepreneur.
3   The legal and investment community has done an excellent job of making much of the critical thinking on these issues as open source as possible. There are a number of excellent books and blogs that provide specific advice to founders and investors in entrepreneurial ventures. Please visit www .patri ckmcginnis.com for a list of helpful resources.

Chapter 8. Building Your Team

1   Networking and entrepreneurship groups exist across the globe. You can get a sense of the breadth of groups that exist in your local geographical area at Meetup.com, which is the world's largest network of local groups and spans many types of interests, including business, investing, and entrepreneurship. Find out more at www.meetup.com/about/.

Chapter 9. Overcoming Obstacles

1   Ben Schreckinger, "The Home of FOMO," *Boston* magazine, Aug. 2014, www.bostonmagazine.com/news/article/2014/07/29/fomo-history/.

Index

Advisors, 45, 48–50
  benefits of, beyond earning
    equity, 50
  combined Advisor/Angel roles, 91
  commitment of time and
    experience by, 49–50
  defined, 207
  documentation for involvement
    as, 143
  due diligence process and, 128
  financial capital supplemented by
    acting as, 90
  resource commitment and, 68–69,
    70–71
  tailoring pitch to different
    audiences, 158
Aficionados, 45, 54–55
  defined, 207
  documentation for involvement
    as, 143
  resource commitment and, 72
AIG, 3–4
Amazon Launchpad, 57

anchor tenants, 122–23, 208
Andreessen, Marc, 23
Angel Capital Association, 70
angel investment groups, 70,
    144–45, 147–48
Angels, 45–48
  amount of investment to make,
    47–48
  average allocation of wealth to
    entrepreneurial activities, 87
  benefits of investing, 48
  combined Advisor/Angel roles, 91
  defined, 208
  diversification and, 91
  documentation for involvement
    as, 143
  due diligence process and, 128
  resource commitment and, 68,
    69–70
  return on investment, expectations
    as to, 89–90
  tailoring pitch to different
    audiences, 158

Index

AngelVest, 147–48
Apple, 15–16
Apple Watch, 170–71

Barlow, Peter, 41–43, 139, 163, 182, 190–91, 202
Bean, William Bao, 147
beer industry, 63–65
Belveal, Todd, 42–43
benefits of 10% entrepreneurship, 24–40
  critical skills development as, 29, 36–38
  enriching life as, 29, 33–36
  ownership, value of, 29, 32–33
  personal interests, integrating, 33–36
  Plan B, downside protection and diversification through having, 28–31
  upside opportunity as, 31–33
Bieber, Justin, 190
biography, preparation of
  credibility, establishing, 106
  exercise for, 107–8
  experiences, summarizing, 105–6
  expertise and intellectual capital, identifying, 106–8
  on LinkedIn, 168
  networking contacts, as source of, 160
  pitch creation and, 155–56
  sample biography, 212–13
Birchbox, 49
Bluesmart, 57, 72, 113, 132, 194
bootlegging policy, 36–37
Boston, 179–80
building 10% entrepreneurship, 57–202
  determining what type of entrepreneur you are, 63–76
  investment process, 75, 115–45
  obstacles, overcoming, 173–83

resources of entrepreneurs (See resources of 10% entrepreneurs)
team, building, 147–171
10% plan, developing (See 10% plan)
values for, 185–202
Bunny, Inc., 27–28, 32, 39, 70–71, 86, 112
business due diligence, 129–33
  checklist of critical questions for, 130–31
  demand/market for product, assessing, 132
  memo or business plan, creating, 131–32
  new people, as opportunity to meet, 132
  returns envisioned for project, determining, 133

Camberos, Marcelo, 116–17, 123, 126, 153–54
Chatah, Omar, 186–87
"Chocolate Rain" (video), 116
Choe, David, 50
cocktail party effect, 201–2
cold calls, 160–61
comfort zone, breaking out of, 191–92
compensation, of full-time entrepreneurs, 19–20
complacency, 11–12
complementarity
  intellectual capital and, 112–14
  time spent on projects and, 85–86
connectivity, in team building, 153–54
Conniff, Ben, 52, 137
Costolo, Dick, 47–48
Coupang, 49
courteousness, in networking, 162–63
Craigslist, 136–37
credibility
  biography and, 106
  online, 167–69

critical skills, developing, 29,
      36–38
critics, 199–201
Crotaz, Gary, 54–55

Diffenderffer, Bill, 42–43
diversification
   enriching and making life more
      interesting and, 29, 33–36
   financial, 87, 90–91
   Plan B as means of career, 29–31
documenting involvement, 121–22,
      143–45
   networking and, 152
   specific documents required, 143
downside protection, 29–31
due diligence, 121, 126–41
   by Angels/Advisors versus
      Founders, 128–29
   on business, 129–33
   checklists for conducting, 130–31,
      135–36, 140–41
   defined, 208
   intellectual capital of your network
      to fill gaps in, 151–52
   networking and, 151–52
   on partners, 133–37
   questions to answer in conducting,
      127–28
   on role you will play in venture,
      137–41
Duggal, Ann, 111

education, 192–94
employer, current. See full-time job/
      employer
empty-calorie e-mails, 161
entrepreneurs/entrepreneurship
   in corporate environment, 36–37
   failure and, 22–23
   financial implications of, 19–20
   glorification of, 14–16
   job market insecurity and, 12–14
   lifestyle of, 18–19

part-time (See 10% entrepreneurship)
   reasons for not being full-time,
      16–23
   right idea for, 21–22
   risk and, 5
   status and affirmation,
      relinquishing, 20–21
   time and focus required for, 18
Entrepreneurship, Inc., 14–16, 208
equity, 208

Fab.com, 49
Facebook, 19, 50
face time, 81–82
failure, 22–23, 175, 182–83
failure fetish, 23
family, partnering with, 86, 160,
      196–97
F Cubed (Female Founders Fund),
      111–12
Female Founders Fund (F Cubed),
      111–12
Ferreira, Beth, 49, 53, 71, 111–12
final decision, 121, 141–43
   checklist for, 142
   networking and, 152
financial capital, 66–72
   Advisor roles as means of
      supplementing, 90–91
   amount to commit, determining,
      86–87
   diversification and, 87, 90–91
   exercise for managing, 88
   freeing up, 87–89
   investing sweat equity when you
      don't have financial capital, 68
   return on investment, expectations
      as to, 89–90
   risk tolerance and, 89, 91
   sample spreadsheets for managing,
      210–11
   10% plan and, 86–92
   type of 10% entrepreneur and,
      69–72

Index

financial implications, of full-time entrepreneurship, 19–20
financial profession, 13
flexibility, 39
FOBO (Fear of a Better Option), 180–81, 208
FODA (Fear of Doing Anything), 180, 208
followership, 119–20
FOMO (Fear of Missing Out), 179–81, 208
Founders, 45, 50–54
  defined, 208
  documentation for involvement as, 143
  due diligence process and, 128–29
  resource commitment and, 71–72
4moms, 191
Foushee, Scott, 134
freelancing, 44–45
full-time job/employer, 2
  integrity in dealing with, 53–54, 188–90
  prioritizing, 82–83

game plan, for 10% entrepreneurship, 73–76
Gertsacov, Dan, 34–35, 72, 113
Ghosh, Shikhar, 23
Golden Rule, 197–98
Google, 37, 45–46, 136, 168, 169
Google test, 168–69
Guerard, Margaux, 170–71

Haim, Gabe, 63–64, 65, 132
Hayati, 186–87
Hodes, Paul, 3
Holden, Bryan, 196
Holden, Luke, 50–54, 72, 111, 112, 132, 136–37, 165, 196
Holden, Michael, 196
Home Depot, 45–46
hub-and-spoke network, 152–53

Huffington Post, 169
Hutton, Timothy, 199

ideas worth risking entrepreneurship for, 21–22, 94–102
  exercise for identifying, 97–98
  integration into life of, 98–102
  investment process for determining (See investment process)
  opportunity cost and, 95
image you project
  obstacles, overcoming, 179
  pitch creation and, 156
impostor syndrome, 176–79
integrating ideas into life, 98–102
integrity, 53–54, 188–90
intellectual capital, 66–72, 91–114
  biography, writing, 105–8
  complementarity and, 112–14
  defined, 208
  ideas for entrepreneurship, identifying and integrating, 21–22, 94–102
  network's, in due diligence process, 151–52
  partnering in areas where you lack, 112–14
  skills and expertise, identifying, 102–8
  specific questions, seeking answers to, 165–67
  strengths, pursuing projects that play to your, 108–14
  of team, 165–67
  type of 10% entrepreneur and, 69–72
investment process, 75, 115–45
  choice of investments, freedom and responsibility in making, 120–21
  documentation phase, 121–22, 143–45, 152
  due diligence and, 121, 126–41, 151–52

final decision and, 121, 141–43, 152
followership and, 119–20
networking and, 151–52
screening process and, 121,
    124–26, 151
sourcing and, 121, 122–24, 151
ipsy, 117–18, 121, 129–30, 142,
    144, 154
Iverson, Joel, 63, 64–65

Jennings, Hillyer, 37, 38, 72, 158,
    194, 196
job market, 11–16
    complacency in, 11–12
    glorification of entrepreneurship
        as alternative to, 14–16
    job security, lack of, 12–14
    Plan B formation as means of
        diversifying risk inherent in,
        28–31
Jobs, Steve, 15

Khan, Farah, 46–47, 53, 111–12, 165
Kickstarter, 170

Langer, William, 202
La Xarcuteria, 35, 113
legal profession, 13
Liberboim, Nir, 117, 153–54
lifestyle, of full-time entrepreneurs,
    18–19
LinkedIn, 106, 108, 136, 160, 168
Linnenbank, Patrick, 77–79, 82, 85,
    156–57
Luke's Lobster, 51, 52–53, 72, 111,
    112, 132

McConaughey, Levi, 101
McConaughey, Matthew, 101
McGinnis, Mike, 16–17
Masala Baby, 100, 101, 102,
    112, 132
Mayes, Michael, 122, 125
Mediatavern, 30–31

medical profession, 13
Meetup groups, 163
Mela Artisans, 101
MEMI, 170–71, 191
mental toughness, and overcoming
    obstacles, 175–76
Mese, Ali, 18
mind-set for entrepreneurship, 80,
    120, 177–78, 185–88
Modem Media, 30
Monday Night Brewing, 63, 64–65,
    86, 132, 139
money. See financial capital
multipolar network, 153–55
multitasking, 81

networking, 75, 145, 147–55,
    159–69
    angel investment group, joining,
        147–48
    broad events for, attending, 163
    cold calls and, 160–61
    courteousness and, 162–63
    database of potential team
        members, creating, 164
    due diligence and, 151–52
    empty-calorie e-mails, avoiding, 161
    existing network, tapping, 160
    guidelines for initiating contacts,
        161–62
    intellectual capital and, 151–52
    investment process and, 151–52
    multipolar versus hub-and-spoke,
        152–55
    online, 167–69
    organized approach to, 163
    persistence in, 162
    screening process and, 151
    sourcing and, 123, 151
    systematic approach to, 159, 163
Newman, Josh, 30, 197
Newman, Lisa, 197
Newton-Tanzer, Gavin, 148–49, 156,
    194–95

Index

obstacles, overcoming, 173–83
  failure, dealing with and learning
    from, 182–83
  FOMA/FOBA and, 179–81
  image you project to world and, 179
  impostor syndrome, avoiding,
    176–79
  mental toughness and, 175–76
  mind-set for entrepreneurship and,
    177–78
  resilience in, 173–76
  10% Plan, trusting in, 181–82
Oi Paggo, 110
Oliver, Mary, 93, 94
Olsen, Jonathan, 19
110% entrepreneurs, 45, 56–57
  defined, 207
  documentation for involvement
    as, 143
  resource commitment and, 72
online networking, 167–69
opportunity cost, 95, 97–98
  calculation of, 95
  defined, 208
  exercise for examining ideas with
    zero, 97–98
ownership, value of, 29, 32–33
Oyster Bay Brewing Company, 63,
    65, 67, 86, 132

P. J. Clarke's, 199
partners, due diligence on, 133–37
  bad partners, potential
    consequences of choosing, 134
  checklist of questions for assessing
    partners, 135–36
  goals and values, selecting
    partners who share your,
    133–34, 195–97
  Google as tool for conducting, 136
  LinkedIn/social network research
    as method for conducting, 136
part-time entrepreneurship. See 10%
  entrepreneurship

Patwa, Dipali, 100–102, 111, 132, 189
PayPal, 45–46
persistence, in networking, 162
personal interests, integrating into
    entrepreneurial ventures, 33–36
Phan, Michelle, 117
Pierson, Leslie, 170–71, 182–83, 191
Pierucci, Tomi, 56–57, 113
pitch, 155–58
  biography and, 155–56
  exercise for crafting, 157–58
  integrating all brands listed on
    resumé into, 158
  tailoring for different audiences, 158
Pixable, 49
plan, for 10% entrepreneurship, 73–76
Plan B, downside protection and
    diversification through having,
    28–31
playing to your strengths strategy,
    108–14, 190–91
Playlist Live conference, 116, 118
Post-It, 36–37
professional biography, preparation
    of. See biography, preparation of

Quarre, Thomas, 167

Ready Steady Mums, 174–75
Real Influence, 116, 117, 118, 123,
    126, 153
rejection, 197–98
reputation, 170–71
resilience, in overcoming obstacles,
    173–76
resources of 10% entrepreneurs,
    77–114
  financial capital (See financial
    capital)
  intellectual capital as (See
    intellectual capital)
  as portfolio, 66–67
  screening process to match
    projects with, 124–25

time (*See* time)
types of 10% entrepreneurs,
    correlation to, 69–72
return on investment, 89–90
risk
    comfort zone, breaking out of,
        191–92
    financial capital commitments
        and, 89, 91
    of full-time entrepreneurship, 5,
        16, 18, 24–25
    10% entrepreneurship as means of
        mitigating, 28, 29–31
Rittes, Roberto, 109–10, 111
role in venture, due diligence on
    checklist for conducting, 140–41
    value you can provide company,
        determining, 138–39

Saez-Gil, Diego, 56–57, 72, 113, 132,
    140, 194
Saverin, Eduardo, 43
Schlotter, Ryan, 63–64, 65
Schreckinger, Ben, 179–80
screening process, 121, 124–26
    first project, tips for selecting,
        125–26
    networking and, 151
    resources and strengths, aligning
        projects with, 124–25
Scraph Protection Group, 78
serial 10% entrepreneurship, 43
70-20-10 model, 37
Shah, Suken, 155
Siegel, Stephen, 198–99
Silicon Valley (TV series), 14
Silvercar, 43, 132, 139, 182, 191
Skybus Airlines, 42
Social Network, The (film), 14
sourcing, 121, 122–24
    anchor tenant concept and, 122–23
    networking and, 123, 151
specific questions, seeking answers
    to, 165–67

Starbucks, 45–46
Steinbrenner, George, 199
strengths
    comfort zone, breaking out of,
        191–92
    identifying, 102–8
    pursuing projects that play to your,
        108–14, 190–91
"Summer Day, The" (Oliver), 93
Sunrise International Education, 148
sweat equity, 6–7, 32, 48, 68, 208

team building, 147–171
    connectivity and, 153–54
    exercise for, 164
    intellectual capital and, 165–67
    knowing where to look for
        answers, 150–55
    multipolar network versus
        hub-and-spoke network,
        building, 152–55
    networking and, 147–55, 159–69
    pitch, creating, 155–58
    reputation and, 170–71
    specific questions, seeking answers
        to, 165–67
10% entrepreneurs/entrepreneurship
    author's journey toward, 2–7
    benefits of (*See* benefits of 10%
        entrepreneurship)
    building (*See* building 10%
        entrepreneurship)
    defined, 2, 207
    flexibility and, 29
    freelancing, distinguished, 44–45
    plan for (*See* 10% plan)
    resources of (*See* resources of 10%
        entrepreneurs)
    tailoring of, to your life, 38–40
    technology enabling, 39–40
    traditional career, as complement
        to, 24–25
    types of (*See* types of 10%
        entrepreneurship)

Index

10% plan, 73–76
  financial capital and, 86–92
  intellectual capital and, 93–114
  investment process and (*See*
    investment process)
  network mobilization and, 147–55,
    159–64
  obstacles, overcoming, 181–82
  team building and (*See* team
    building)
  time and, 80–86
Teten, David, 90
3M, 36–37
time, 66–72, 80–86
  achieving multiple objectives during
    one fixed period and, 81–83
  combining passive activities with
    those requiring deeper thinking
    and, 81
  complementarity and, 85–86
  distractions, eliminating, 83–84
  eliminating activities that do not
    fit with priorities and, 83–85
  exercise for managing, 84
  face time, mastering, 81–82
  prioritization and, 83–85
  10% Plan and, 80–86
  type of 10% entrepreneur and, 69–72
Torrenegra, Alex, 27–28, 32, 39, 112,
  191–92, 197
Tuncer, Katy, 173–75, 182–83
Twitter, 47–48
types of 10% entrepreneurship,
  41–59
  Advisors, 45, 48–50, 70–71
  Aficionados, 45, 54–55, 72
  Angels, 45–48, 69–70
  determining your type, 63–76
  Founders, 45, 50–54, 71–72
  110% entrepreneurs, 45, 56–57, 72
  resource commitment and, 69–72
  serial, 43

unanswered questions, seeking
  answers to, 165–67
upside opportunity, 31–33
Upwork, 39
USA Today, 57

values and principles of 10%
  entrepreneurship, 185–202
  critics, avoid wasting time
    convincing, 199–201
  educating oneself, 192–94
  Golden Rule, following,
    197–98
  integrity, acting with, 188–90
  interests as element of
    entrepreneurship, 201–2
  mind-set for entrepreneurship and,
    185–88
  ongoing and dynamic part of life,
    entrepreneurship as, 198–99
  playing to your strength strategy,
    190–91
  spreading wealth, 194–95
  working with people who share
    your values, 195–97
Vlasic, Mark, 105

Wall Street (film), 14
WeHostels, 56, 140
WeWork, 39
Williams, Evan, 47–48
Wozniak, Steve, 15–16
Wrist Tunes, 37, 38, 72, 194

Y Combinator, 57
Youtube, 116
Yuan, Mildred, 54–55

Zapata, Tania, 27–28, 39, 112,
  192, 197
Zonday, Tay, 116
Zuckerberg, Mark, 14